DATA DIVERSITY IN AI AND EMERGING TECHNOLOGIES

Creating Robust, Ethical, And Impactful AI Systems That Serve Diverse Global Needs Effectively

DR. IVAN DEL VALLE

Printed in the United States of America

ISBN: 979-8-304-74296-2

First Edition

To my beloved wife, Ruth Elaine Sus,

Thirty-one years of marriage have only deepened the mystery of how two souls can become one. In your eyes, I see a love that has grown more profound with each passing day. Your touch ignites a flame that burns brighter with every kiss, every whisper, and every promise. You are the melody that fills my heart with joy, the rhythm that makes me whole.

With every sunrise, I am reminded of the gift that you are to me. Your love is a masterpiece, crafted with patience, kindness, and devotion. You are the safe haven where I can be myself, where I can find solace in your embracing arms. Your presence in my life is a testament to the power of true love, a love that has stood the test of time and has only grown stronger.

Through laughter and tears, through triumphs and tribulations, you have been my rock, my guiding star. Your unwavering support and encouragement have given me the courage to chase my dreams, to pursue my passions. You are the missing piece that makes me complete, the missing beat that makes my heart sing.

As we journey through life together, I am constantly amazed by the depth of your love, the breadth of your compassion, and the beauty of your spirit. You are a ray of sunshine that brightens every day, a gentle breeze that soothes my soul. You are my forever love, my soulmate, my everything.

To you, my dear Ruth, I offer my eternal gratitude, my deepest love, and my heartfelt devotion. May our love continue to flourish, may our bond continue to strengthen, and may our hearts continue to beat as one. Forever and always, my love.

With all my love and devotion, your husband,

Ivan

CONTENTS

ACKNOWLEDGMENTS

The journey of life is filled with moments of triumph and struggle, joy and hardship. Yet, it is in these moments that we are reminded of the profound impact that kindness, compassion, and connection can have on our lives. The words of encouragement, the listening ears, and the supportive hearts of those around us have the power to uplift, to inspire, and to transform.

As we navigate the complexities of life, it is easy to feel isolated, alone, or disconnected from the world around us. But it is in these moments that we must remember that we are not forgotten. We are not alone. There are those who see us, who hear us, and who care deeply about our well-being. May the kindness of strangers, the love of friends and family, and the warmth of community envelop us, reminding us of our worth, our value, and our place in this world.

The holiday season is a time for celebration, a time for joy, and a time for connection. It is a time to remember the power of small gestures, the impact of kindness, and the importance of reaching out to those around us. May we take a moment to remind those in our lives of their importance, their value, and their place in our hearts. May we offer a listening ear, a comforting word, or a helping hand.

As we come together to celebrate the holiday season, may we be mindful of the impact that our words and actions can have on those around us. May we strive to create a sense of community, of belonging, and of connection that transcends our differences and unites us in our shared humanity.

Happy Holidays to all. May your heart be filled with joy, love, and all the things that bring you peace. May you be surrounded by the love of friends and family, and may you be reminded of your worth, your value, and your place in this world.

Sincerely,

Dr. Ivan Del Valle

INTRODUCTION

As we reflect on the journey through the intricate landscape of data diversity in AI and emerging technologies, it becomes evident that the quest for robust, ethical, and impactful AI systems is both a challenge and a necessity. The diversity of data is not just a technical requirement but a moral imperative, shaping systems that are fair, inclusive, and reflective of the world's multifaceted nature. In the pursuit of this goal, we have explored the vital importance of ensuring that AI models are trained on datasets that encompass a rich variety of demographics, languages, cultures, and environments. This diversity is crucial to minimizing bias, enhancing generalization, and fostering innovation across different domains. The challenges we face, from bias in data collection to the cost and complexity of managing diverse datasets, are significant. Yet, they are surmountable through strategic approaches such as inclusive data sourcing, the use of synthetic data, and cross-domain collaborations. These strategies not only mitigate biases but also pave the way for more resilient and adaptable AI systems. As AI continues to permeate various sectors like healthcare, autonomous systems, and natural language processing, the demand for data diversity will only grow. It is essential for stakeholders to engage in ongoing dialogue, ensuring ethical governance and compliance with regulations. By embracing data diversity, we are not only advancing technology but also contributing to a more equitable society, where AI serves the diverse needs of global populations effectively. The path forward is

one of collaboration, innovation, and steadfast commitment to ethical
principles, ensuring that the benefits of AI are shared widely and justly.

Chapter 1: Understanding Data Diversity
Definition and Importance

Data diversity is a critical concept in the field of artificial intelligence (AI) and emerging technologies. It refers to the inclusion of a wide variety of data types used in the training, validation, and testing phases of AI models. This diversity encompasses numerous dimensions such as demographics, languages, cultures, environments, and scenarios. The goal is to ensure that AI systems are inclusive, fair, and effective across different populations, thereby minimizing bias and enhancing the robustness of these systems.

The importance of data diversity cannot be overstated. It ensures that AI systems are not only more inclusive but also more capable of generalizing across diverse real-world scenarios. A lack of diversity in data can lead to biased AI models that may perform well on certain groups or scenarios but fail when applied to others. This limitation can have significant consequences, especially when AI systems are used in critical areas such as healthcare, law enforcement, and finance.

There are several types of diversity that are crucial for AI systems. Demographic diversity includes factors such as age, gender, ethnicity, socioeconomic status, and geographic location. Contextual diversity involves variations in environments such as urban versus rural settings, as well as different cultural contexts and use cases. Temporal diversity refers to data collected over different time periods to capture trends and seasonality. Domain-specific diversity includes variations in industry-specific data, such as healthcare records, manufacturing sensors, or educational datasets.

However, achieving data diversity is not without its challenges. Bias in data collection can arise due to the underrepresentation of certain groups or scenarios, which may be a result of systemic issues or limited access to data sources. Additionally, there is often a scarcity of diverse, high-quality datasets in specialized domains. The cost and complexity of gathering and managing diverse datasets can also be prohibitive. Moreover, regulatory and privacy constraints pose significant challenges, as accessing sensitive or protected data often involves navigating complex legal and ethical considerations.

Despite these challenges, the benefits of data diversity are substantial. Improved generalization is one of the primary advantages, as models trained on diverse data perform better across a range of real-world scenarios. It also helps in bias mitigation, ensuring fairness in decision-making processes. Furthermore, diverse data can drive enhanced innovation by inspiring novel applications and insights. AI systems that are trained on a wide variety of data are also more resilient to edge cases, meaning they are better equipped to handle rare or unexpected inputs.

To promote data diversity, several strategies can be employed. Inclusive data sourcing involves actively seeking out data from underrepresented groups and contexts. When real-world data is limited, synthetic data can be used to simulate diverse scenarios. Cross-domain collaboration with organizations across different industries and regions can also help in accessing varied datasets. Regular bias auditing and the use of metrics can help evaluate datasets for gaps and biases. Federated learning is another approach that leverages decentralized data sources while maintaining privacy and security.

In conclusion, data diversity is foundational for creating robust, ethical, and impactful AI systems that can effectively serve the diverse needs of a global population. By addressing the challenges and implementing strategies to enhance data diversity, AI and emerging technologies can be developed to be more inclusive, fair, and effective.

Types of Diversity

In the realm of artificial intelligence and emerging technologies, the concept of data diversity plays a pivotal role in shaping models that are both inclusive and robust. Demographic diversity encompasses a wide array of factors such as age, gender, ethnicity, socioeconomic status, and geographic location. This type of diversity is crucial in ensuring that AI systems do not inadvertently perpetuate biases or exclude segments of the population. By integrating diverse demographic data, these systems can be trained to recognize and respect the nuances present in different groups, leading to fairer outcomes.

Contextual diversity is another vital facet, focusing on variations in environments, cultures, and specific use cases. AI models must be exposed to data from both urban and rural settings, as well as different cultural backgrounds, to function effectively across various contexts. This diversity allows AI systems to adapt more seamlessly to distinct scenarios, enhancing their applicability and reliability in a multitude of environments.

Temporal diversity involves the collection of data over different time periods, capturing trends and seasonal variations. This type of diversity is essential for models that need to predict or react to time-sensitive information, such as economic forecasts or climate models. Temporal diversity ensures that AI systems can adjust to changes over time, maintaining their accuracy and relevance.

Domain-specific diversity refers to the variations in data specific to certain industries or fields, like healthcare records, manufacturing sensors, or educational datasets. This diversity is critical for developing AI models tailored to address the unique challenges and requirements of different sectors. By leveraging domain-specific data, AI technologies can provide more precise insights and solutions.

While the importance of data diversity is clear, achieving it poses several challenges. Bias in data collection can lead to the underrepresentation of certain groups, often due to systemic issues or limited access to comprehensive data sources. Additionally, the availability of diverse, high-quality datasets can be scarce, particularly in specialized domains. The cost and complexity of gathering and managing such datasets can also be prohibitive, requiring significant resources and expertise.

7

Furthermore, regulatory and privacy constraints add another layer of complexity. Legal and ethical considerations must be addressed when accessing sensitive or protected data, ensuring compliance with regulations and maintaining the trust of data subjects. Despite these challenges, the pursuit of data diversity is integral to the development of fair, effective, and innovative AI systems.

The benefits of data diversity are manifold. It enhances the generalization of models, enabling them to perform well across diverse real-world scenarios. By reducing algorithmic bias, data diversity ensures fairness in decision-making processes, fostering trust and acceptance of AI technologies. Additionally, it drives innovation by providing a broader dataset that inspires new applications and insights. AI systems also become more resilient to edge cases, equipped to handle rare or unexpected inputs, thus increasing their robustness and reliability.

To promote data diversity, several strategies can be employed. Inclusive data sourcing aims to actively seek data from underrepresented groups and contexts. When real-world data is limited, synthetic data generated through models can simulate diverse scenarios. Cross-domain collaboration with organizations across industries and regions can provide access to varied datasets. Regular bias auditing and metrics evaluation help identify and address gaps in datasets, ensuring continuous improvement. Federated learning, which leverages decentralized data sources while maintaining privacy, offers

8

a promising approach to enhancing data diversity without compromising security.

Challenges in Achieving Diversity

Achieving diversity in data for AI and emerging technologies presents a multifaceted challenge. Central to this issue is the bias inherent in data collection. Often, certain groups or scenarios are underrepresented due to systemic issues or limited access to data sources, leading to datasets that do not accurately reflect the diversity of the real world. This underrepresentation can result in AI models that are biased, as they are trained on incomplete or skewed data sets.

Another significant challenge is data availability. In many specialized domains, there is a scarcity of diverse, high-quality datasets. This lack of availability can impede the development of AI technologies that are robust and effective across different contexts. For example, in healthcare, the absence of diverse medical records can lead to diagnostic models that perform poorly across varied patient demographics.

The cost and complexity of gathering and managing diverse datasets further complicate efforts to achieve data diversity. Collecting data from a wide range of sources and ensuring its quality requires substantial resources. This process is not only time-consuming but also requires significant financial investment, which can be prohibitive for many organizations.

Moreover, regulatory and privacy constraints pose additional hurdles. Accessing sensitive or protected data is often subject to strict legal and ethical guidelines, which can limit the scope of data that can be collected and used. These constraints are critical in ensuring that data collection practices respect individuals' rights and maintain trust, yet they also restrict the breadth of data diversity that can be achieved.

Despite these challenges, the pursuit of data diversity is essential for the development of AI systems that are fair, inclusive, and effective. Diverse data improves model generalization, allowing AI systems to perform better across various real-world scenarios. It also helps mitigate bias, ensuring that decision-making processes are fair and equitable. Furthermore, diverse datasets can inspire innovation, leading to novel applications and insights that might not have been possible with more homogenous data.

To address these challenges, several strategies can be employed. Inclusive data sourcing involves actively seeking out data from underrepresented groups and contexts, thereby broadening the diversity of the dataset. The use of synthetic data, generated by models to simulate diverse scenarios, can also be a valuable tool when real-world data is limited.

Cross-domain collaboration is another effective strategy, where partnerships with organizations across different industries and regions can provide access to varied datasets. Additionally, bias auditing and metrics can be employed to regularly evaluate datasets for gaps and

10

biases, ensuring that they are as comprehensive and representative as possible.

Federated learning offers a way to leverage decentralized data sources while maintaining privacy and security. This approach allows for the use of diverse datasets without the need to centralize sensitive information, thus navigating the regulatory and privacy constraints that often limit data diversity efforts.

In summary, while achieving data diversity in AI and emerging technologies is fraught with challenges, it is a critical endeavor. By addressing issues related to bias, data availability, cost, complexity, and regulatory constraints, and by employing strategic solutions, it is possible to develop AI systems that are truly reflective of the diverse world they are meant to serve.

Benefits of Diversity

Data diversity plays a crucial role in the development and deployment of artificial intelligence (AI) and emerging technologies, offering numerous advantages that contribute to the robustness, fairness, and effectiveness of these systems. One of the primary benefits of incorporating diverse data is the improved generalization of AI models. When trained on a wide array of data that reflects the complexity of real-world scenarios, these models are better equipped to perform accurately across different environments and populations, thereby enhancing their applicability and reliability.

Another significant advantage is the mitigation of bias, a persistent challenge in AI systems. By ensuring that data encompasses a broad spectrum of demographic, contextual, and temporal elements, the risk of algorithmic bias is substantially reduced. This leads to fairer decision-making processes and outcomes, as the AI is less likely to favor any particular group or scenario over others. The diverse data sets act as a safeguard against the inadvertent perpetuation of biases that could arise from homogeneous data sources.

Diversity in data also spurs innovation by providing a richer foundation for discovering novel applications and insights. When AI systems are exposed to diverse datasets, they can uncover patterns and opportunities that might remain hidden in more limited datasets. This can lead to breakthroughs in various fields, from healthcare to marketing, where understanding and leveraging subtle variations can drive significant advancements.

Furthermore, AI systems built on diverse data are more resilient to edge cases, which are rare or unexpected inputs that can cause systems to fail. By training on a diverse set of scenarios, these systems become more adept at handling a wide range of inputs, reducing the likelihood of errors in unpredictable situations. This resilience is particularly important in critical applications such as autonomous vehicles or healthcare, where the cost of failure can be high.

To harness these benefits effectively, several strategies can be employed to promote data diversity. Inclusive data sourcing is one approach, which involves actively seeking out data from underrepresented groups and contexts to ensure a comprehensive data set. Additionally, synthetic data generation can be utilized to simulate diverse scenarios, especially when real-world data is scarce or difficult to obtain. Collaborations across different domains and industries also facilitate access to varied datasets, enriching the data pool available for AI training.

Regular bias auditing and the use of specialized metrics can help identify gaps and biases in datasets, allowing for continuous refinement and improvement. Federated learning, which leverages decentralized data sources while maintaining privacy, is another innovative approach that supports data diversity without compromising security.

In conclusion, the integration of diverse data is not merely a technical consideration but a foundational principle for developing ethical, robust, and impactful AI systems. By embracing diversity, AI technologies can better serve the global population, addressing a wide array of needs and challenges with fairness and accuracy.

Strategies for Promoting Diversity

Promoting diversity in data for AI and emerging technologies is vital to ensure the development of inclusive, fair, and effective systems. One of the primary strategies is inclusive data sourcing, which involves actively seeking data from underrepresented groups and contexts. This approach helps mitigate biases that arise from underrepresentation and ensures that AI systems are trained on a wide variety of data reflective of the real world.

Another key strategy is the use of synthetic data. By utilizing generative models, researchers can simulate diverse scenarios, particularly when real-world data is scarce or difficult to obtain. Synthetic data can fill the gaps in existing datasets, providing a broader spectrum of inputs for AI models. This not only aids in bias reduction but also enhances the robustness of AI systems.

Cross-domain collaboration is also crucial. By partnering with organizations across different industries and regions, it is possible to access varied datasets that cover a wide range of scenarios and demographics. This collaborative approach broadens the scope of data diversity, facilitating the creation of models that perform well across different contexts and use cases.

Bias auditing and metrics are essential components in promoting data diversity. Regular evaluation of datasets for gaps and biases using specialized tools and frameworks ensures that the data used in AI training is as comprehensive and balanced as possible. This ongoing auditing process helps identify and rectify potential biases, leading to more equitable AI outcomes.

Federated learning offers a novel approach to leveraging decentralized data sources while maintaining privacy and security. By allowing AI models to be trained on local data sources without the need to centralize the data, federated learning respects privacy constraints and enables the inclusion of diverse data from various locations. This method enhances the diversity of data without compromising individual privacy.

The implementation of these strategies is critical in areas such as healthcare, where diverse medical records can significantly improve diagnostic accuracy across different populations. In autonomous systems, diverse environmental data enhances safety and adaptability, ensuring that these systems can function effectively in varied conditions. Similarly, in natural language processing, multilingual and culturally varied data improve language models, making them more applicable to global audiences. In retail and marketing, diverse consumer data supports the creation of personalized experiences that cater to a global customer base.

Ethical and governance considerations are integral to these strategies. Adhering to ethical principles such as fairness, accountability, and transparency is essential. Compliance with data protection regulations, like GDPR and CCPA, ensures that data diversity efforts respect legal standards. Additionally, fostering stakeholder engagement helps address societal impacts and build trust in AI systems. By integrating these strategies, the goal is to develop AI technologies that are not only technically proficient but also ethically responsible and socially beneficial, meeting the diverse needs of a global population.

Chapter 2: Demographic Diversity
Age and Gender

In the realm of artificial intelligence and emerging technologies, the consideration of age and gender in data diversity is pivotal to developing systems that are equitable and effective across diverse demographic groups. The interplay between age and gender within datasets serves as a crucial factor in shaping AI models that mirror the multifaceted nature of society. This aspect of data diversity encompasses a wide range of challenges and opportunities that are essential for creating robust AI systems.

Age diversity in AI data sets refers to the inclusion of data from individuals across different age groups. This is critical because age can significantly influence behavior, preferences, and needs, which in turn affect how individuals interact with technology. For instance, younger users might be more adept at using digital interfaces and more open to adopting new technologies, while older users might prioritize ease of use and accessibility. By ensuring that datasets include a broad spectrum of ages, AI systems can be designed to cater to the varied needs of these groups, enhancing user experience and accessibility.

Gender diversity is another fundamental component of data diversity. Gender influences a multitude of social dynamics and personal experiences, affecting how individuals engage with technology. Historically, gender bias in data collection and AI model training has led to systems that disproportionately favor one gender over others, often marginalizing non-binary, transgender, and female users. This has been observed in various applications, from voice recognition software that performs better with male voices to recruitment algorithms that favor male candidates. By actively incorporating gender diversity into AI datasets, developers can mitigate these biases, ensuring that AI systems are fair and inclusive.

The integration of age and gender diversity into AI systems is not without challenges. One major hurdle is the underrepresentation of certain age and gender groups in existing datasets. This can be attributed to systemic biases in data collection processes, where certain groups may have less access to technology or may be less likely to participate in data-generating activities. Additionally, there are ethical and privacy concerns associated with collecting sensitive demographic information, which must be navigated carefully to protect individuals' rights.

Despite these challenges, the benefits of incorporating age and gender diversity in AI are substantial. Diverse datasets can lead to improved model generalization, allowing AI systems to perform better across a variety of real-world scenarios. This diversity also helps reduce algorithmic bias, promoting fairness and equality in AI-driven decision-making processes. Moreover, by understanding and anticipating the needs of different demographic groups, AI systems can inspire innovative solutions tailored to diverse user bases.

To effectively incorporate age and gender diversity, several strategies can be employed. Inclusive data sourcing is crucial, involving efforts to actively seek out data from underrepresented groups. Synthetic data generation can also be a valuable tool, allowing the simulation of diverse scenarios when real-world data is scarce. Furthermore, cross-domain collaboration can facilitate access to varied datasets, while bias auditing and metrics help ensure continuous evaluation and improvement of data diversity.

Ultimately, the integration of age and gender diversity in AI is a vital step toward developing technologies that are not only technically proficient but also socially responsible and attuned to the needs of all users. By prioritizing these aspects of diversity, the AI community can contribute to a future where technology serves as an equalizer, bridging gaps and fostering inclusivity across the globe.

Ethnicity and Culture

In the realm of artificial intelligence and emerging technologies, the consideration of ethnicity and culture holds significant importance. These factors profoundly influence the design, development, and deployment of AI systems, impacting their fairness, inclusivity, and effectiveness. Understanding the nuances of ethnicity and culture is crucial for creating technologies that are not only innovative but also equitable and accessible to diverse populations globally.

Ethnicity, as a component of data diversity, encompasses the shared attributes, language, history, and cultural practices of a group. It plays a pivotal role in shaping individual and collective identities. In AI, recognizing ethnic diversity means acknowledging the varied perspectives and experiences that different ethnic groups bring to the table. This recognition ensures that AI systems are trained on datasets that reflect a broad spectrum of human experiences, minimizing biases that could arise from a homogeneous data pool.

Cultural diversity, on the other hand, refers to the myriad ways in which societies express themselves through traditions, customs, and values. In the context of AI, cultural diversity impacts how technologies are perceived and utilized across different regions. For instance, an AI application designed for healthcare must consider cultural differences in medical practices, health beliefs, and patient interaction norms to be truly effective and accepted by users from diverse backgrounds.

The integration of ethnicity and culture into AI systems necessitates a comprehensive approach to data collection and analysis. It begins with inclusive data sourcing strategies that actively seek to represent underrepresented groups. This approach helps in capturing the rich tapestry of human diversity, allowing AI models to generalize better across various demographic and cultural contexts. Furthermore, employing methods like synthetic data generation can simulate diverse scenarios, filling gaps where real-world data might be scarce or difficult to obtain.

19

Challenges in incorporating ethnic and cultural diversity into AI arise from biases in data collection and processing. These biases can stem from systemic issues, such as the underrepresentation of certain groups, or from the inherent limitations of existing datasets. Addressing these challenges requires rigorous bias auditing and the implementation of metrics that evaluate the fairness and inclusivity of AI systems. By doing so, developers can identify and mitigate biases that might otherwise perpetuate inequality or discrimination.

Moreover, cross-domain collaboration is essential to enhance the diversity of data used in AI. By partnering with organizations across different sectors and regions, AI developers can access varied datasets that enrich the training and validation processes. This collaboration fosters innovation and ensures that AI technologies are adaptable to a wide range of cultural settings and ethnic backgrounds.

Ultimately, the consideration of ethnicity and culture in AI is not merely a technical challenge but an ethical imperative. It aligns with broader societal goals of fairness, accountability, and transparency in technology development. By embedding these considerations into the core of AI systems, we pave the way for technologies that respect human diversity and promote social good. This approach not only enhances the performance and acceptance of AI applications but also contributes to building trust and fostering a more inclusive digital future.

Socioeconomic Status

Socioeconomic status (SES) is a complex construct that encompasses an individual's or group's economic and social position in relation to others, based on income, education, and occupation. In the context of AI and emerging technologies, SES plays a critical role in shaping how individuals interact with digital systems, access technology, and benefit from its advancements. Understanding the implications of SES in AI is essential for creating systems that are equitable and accessible to all.

The integration of socioeconomic factors into AI systems is crucial for several reasons. First, SES influences access to technology and digital literacy, which can create disparities in how different groups benefit from technology. For instance, individuals from lower socioeconomic backgrounds might have limited access to the internet and digital devices, which hinders their ability to engage with and benefit from AI-driven services. This digital divide can exacerbate existing inequalities, making it imperative for developers to consider SES when designing and deploying AI systems.

Moreover, SES can affect the quality of data used in training AI models. Data collected from individuals of varying socioeconomic backgrounds can differ significantly in terms of volume, variety, and veracity. For example, health data from affluent communities might be more comprehensive due to better access to healthcare facilities and digital health records, compared to data from underprivileged areas where healthcare access is limited. This disparity can lead to biased AI models that perform well on data from higher SES groups but poorly on data from lower SES groups, thereby perpetuating inequality.

To address these challenges, it is essential to adopt strategies that promote inclusivity and diversity in data collection. This includes actively seeking data from underrepresented socioeconomic groups, employing methods like data augmentation and synthetic data generation to fill gaps, and engaging in cross-sector collaborations to enrich datasets. Furthermore, AI systems should be designed with mechanisms to identify and mitigate biases related to SES, ensuring that outputs are fair and unbiased across different socioeconomic groups.

Incorporating SES considerations into AI development not only enhances the fairness and effectiveness of AI systems but also drives innovation. By understanding and addressing the unique needs and challenges faced by different socioeconomic groups, developers can create more personalized and impactful technologies. For example, AI applications tailored to improve educational outcomes for students from low-income families can lead to significant social benefits and economic growth.

In conclusion, socioeconomic status is a vital factor in the development and deployment of AI and emerging technologies. By acknowledging and addressing SES-related disparities, we can ensure that AI systems are not only technically robust but also socially equitable. This approach is essential for harnessing the full potential of AI to improve lives and create a more inclusive digital future.

Geographic Location

In the context of AI and emerging technologies, geographic location plays a crucial role in shaping the diversity of data used in training, validating, and testing models. The geographic diversity of data encompasses variations in cultural, environmental, and socio-economic factors that are inherently tied to specific locations. These factors influence how data is generated, collected, and interpreted, making geographic location a fundamental aspect of data diversity.

The significance of geographic diversity lies in its ability to enhance the inclusiveness and fairness of AI systems. By incorporating data from a wide array of geographic locations, AI models can better capture the nuances and complexities of different environments and cultures. This leads to more robust models that perform well across various settings, thus minimizing biases that may arise from location-specific data.

One of the primary challenges in achieving geographic diversity in data is the underrepresentation of certain regions, especially those in developing countries or remote areas. These regions often lack the infrastructure and resources necessary for comprehensive data collection, leading to gaps in the datasets available for AI development. This underrepresentation can result in AI systems that are less effective or even biased when deployed in these areas, as the models may not have been exposed to the unique characteristics present in the data from these locations.

To address these challenges, strategies such as inclusive data sourcing and cross-domain collaboration can be employed. Inclusive data sourcing involves actively seeking out data from underrepresented regions and ensuring that these datasets are integrated into AI training processes. Cross-domain collaboration, on the other hand, involves partnering with organizations across different regions and industries to access a broader range of datasets. These strategies not only help fill the geographic data gaps but also promote a more comprehensive understanding of global data diversity.

Moreover, the use of synthetic data and federated learning presents innovative solutions to enhance geographic diversity. Synthetic data, generated through advanced algorithms, can simulate scenarios from underrepresented regions, providing a viable alternative when real-world data is scarce. Federated learning, which involves training AI models across decentralized data sources, allows for the inclusion of data from diverse geographic locations while maintaining data privacy and security.

The benefits of incorporating geographic diversity in AI systems are manifold. Improved generalization is one of the key advantages, as models trained on geographically diverse datasets are better equipped to handle real-world scenarios that vary across different locations. This is particularly important for applications in healthcare, autonomous systems, and natural language processing, where geographic variations can significantly impact model performance.

In addition to technical benefits, geographic diversity in data also aligns with ethical and governance considerations. Ensuring that AI systems are fair and unbiased requires a commitment to representing diverse geographic locations in the datasets used for model development. This not only enhances the ethical standing of AI technologies but also fosters trust among stakeholders, who are increasingly concerned about the societal impacts of AI.

Overall, geographic location is a pivotal factor in the pursuit of data diversity within AI and emerging technologies. By prioritizing geographic diversity, the industry can develop more inclusive, fair, and impactful AI systems that cater to the diverse needs of a global population.

Case Studies

The exploration of data diversity through practical examples provides invaluable insights into its role in shaping AI and emerging technologies. Various industries have embarked on integrating diverse data sets to enhance the efficacy and fairness of AI systems. Healthcare, for instance, exemplifies the critical necessity of data diversity. In this sector, diverse datasets encompassing demographic variables such as age, gender, and ethnicity are crucial in developing AI models that provide accurate and unbiased diagnostics and treatment recommendations across different population groups. The inclusion of varied medical records ensures that AI systems do not disproportionately favor or neglect any group, thus promoting equitable healthcare outcomes.

In the realm of autonomous systems, particularly autonomous vehicles, the significance of data diversity becomes evident. These systems require extensive datasets that capture a wide array of environmental conditions, from urban to rural landscapes, and include diverse weather patterns and traffic scenarios. Such diversity ensures that autonomous systems can function robustly and safely in any setting, reducing the risk of accidents due to unforeseen circumstances. By training on diverse datasets, these systems learn to navigate complex environments and make real-time decisions that account for variability in their operational contexts.

Natural Language Processing (NLP) is another area where data diversity plays a pivotal role. Language models benefit immensely from datasets that encompass multiple languages and dialects, as well as cultural contexts. This diversity allows NLP systems to understand and generate text that is contextually relevant and sensitive to cultural nuances. For instance, a language model trained on a linguistically diverse dataset can accurately interpret idiomatic expressions or slang terms used in different regions, thereby improving user interaction and satisfaction.

The retail and marketing sectors also leverage data diversity to tailor personalized experiences for a global audience. By analyzing diverse consumer data, businesses can identify unique purchasing patterns and preferences across different demographic groups. This enables the creation of targeted marketing strategies that resonate with various cultural and social backgrounds, enhancing customer engagement and loyalty.

Despite the clear advantages, achieving data diversity is fraught with challenges. The underrepresentation of certain groups in datasets can lead to biased AI models that perpetuate existing inequalities. Moreover, the collection and management of diverse datasets can be resource-intensive, requiring substantial investment in terms of time and technology. To address these challenges, strategies such as inclusive data sourcing and the use of synthetic data are employed. Inclusive data sourcing involves actively seeking out data from underrepresented groups, while synthetic data generation uses advanced algorithms to simulate diverse scenarios, thus filling gaps in real-world data.

Cross-domain collaboration is another strategy that enhances data diversity. By partnering with organizations across different industries and regions, companies can access a broader range of datasets, fostering innovation and improving AI model performance. Additionally, regular bias auditing and the implementation of federated learning approaches help maintain data diversity while ensuring privacy and security.

Through these case studies, the transformative potential of data diversity in AI and emerging technologies is evident. It not only enhances the performance and fairness of AI systems but also drives innovation by inspiring new applications and insights. As industries continue to embrace data diversity, the development of robust, ethical, and inclusive AI systems becomes increasingly achievable.

Chapter 3: Contextual Diversity
Urban and Rural Environments

The integration of data diversity within AI systems is essential, particularly when considering the stark contrasts between urban and rural environments. These environments provide distinct datasets that are crucial for training AI models to ensure they are robust and effective across different scenarios. Urban areas, characterized by dense populations, varied infrastructure, and rapid technological advancements, generate a vast amount of data that reflects complex social dynamics and economic activities. This data often includes diverse demographic information, such as age, ethnicity, and socioeconomic status, which is vital for developing AI systems that are fair and inclusive.

Conversely, rural environments offer a different set of data characteristics. These areas may have less technological infrastructure and lower population densities, which can result in a scarcity of data. However, the data from rural settings is equally important as it captures unique environmental and cultural contexts that are not present in urban datasets. This includes information related to agricultural practices, local languages, and traditional customs. By incorporating data from both urban and rural areas, AI technologies can become more adaptable and sensitive to the needs of diverse populations.

Data diversity in urban and rural contexts also poses challenges. In urban settings, the challenge lies in managing the sheer volume and complexity of data, which can be resource-intensive. There is also the risk of over-representing urban data, leading to AI models that may not perform well in rural scenarios. In rural areas, the main challenge is the limited availability of data, which can hinder the development of AI systems that are effective in these environments. To address these issues, strategies such as inclusive data sourcing and synthetic data generation are employed. These methods help in creating balanced datasets that reflect both urban and rural realities.

The benefits of achieving data diversity across urban and rural environments are significant. AI systems that are trained on diverse datasets are better at generalizing across different settings, reducing bias and improving fairness. This is particularly important in applications such as healthcare, where AI models need to be accurate and reliable for patients in both urban hospitals and rural clinics. Additionally, diverse datasets inspire innovation, leading to AI solutions that are more creative and effective.

Promoting data diversity involves cross-domain collaboration and the use of federated learning techniques. By partnering with organizations across various regions and sectors, it is possible to access a wide range of datasets that enhance the diversity of training data. Federated learning allows for decentralized data collection, preserving privacy while ensuring that AI models benefit from diverse inputs.

In conclusion, understanding and implementing data diversity in urban and rural environments is fundamental to the development of AI systems that are equitable and efficient. By acknowledging the unique contributions of both settings, AI technologies can be designed to serve the needs of all communities, fostering inclusion and innovation across the board.

Cultural Variations

Understanding cultural variations is crucial in the realm of artificial intelligence and emerging technologies, where data diversity plays a pivotal role. In the context of AI development, cultural diversity encompasses the inclusion of data from various cultural backgrounds, ensuring that AI systems are not only inclusive but also effective across different cultural settings. This diversity is integral in minimizing biases that may arise from homogeneous data sets, thus enhancing the robustness and fairness of AI models.

Cultural variations in data can manifest in numerous ways, such as differences in language, social norms, values, and communication styles. These variations necessitate a comprehensive approach to data collection and model training, ensuring that AI systems can understand and process inputs from a wide range of cultural contexts. By incorporating culturally diverse data, AI technologies can be tailored to meet the needs of global populations, fostering inclusivity and equity in technological advancement.

One of the primary challenges in achieving cultural diversity in AI is the bias inherent in data collection. Often, data sets are skewed towards dominant cultures, leading to underrepresentation of minority groups. This imbalance can result in AI systems that are less effective or even discriminatory when applied in diverse cultural contexts. To address this issue, it is essential to adopt strategies that actively seek out and include data from underrepresented cultural groups. This may involve collaborating with local communities and organizations to gain access to culturally specific data and insights.

Moreover, cultural variations can impact the interpretation and application of AI models. For example, natural language processing (NLP) systems must be trained on multilingual and culturally varied data to accurately understand and generate human language across different cultures. Similarly, AI applications in healthcare must consider cultural differences in medical practices and patient interactions to provide equitable healthcare solutions globally.

Incorporating cultural diversity also enhances the innovation potential of AI technologies. Diverse cultural perspectives can inspire novel applications and insights, driving the development of AI solutions that are more adaptable and responsive to the needs of different communities. Furthermore, AI systems that are resilient to cultural edge cases are better equipped to handle rare or unexpected inputs, thereby improving their overall performance and reliability.

To promote cultural diversity in AI, several strategies can be employed. These include inclusive data sourcing, where efforts are made to gather data from a wide range of cultural contexts, and the use of synthetic data to simulate diverse scenarios when real-world data is limited. Additionally, cross-domain collaboration with international partners can provide access to culturally diverse data sets, while bias auditing and metrics can help identify and address gaps in cultural representation.

Ultimately, the goal of integrating cultural variations into AI development is to create systems that reflect the diverse tapestry of human society. By doing so, we can ensure that AI technologies are not only technologically advanced but also socially responsible, promoting a future where technology serves all of humanity equitably.

Use Cases in Different Contexts

In the rapidly evolving landscape of artificial intelligence (AI) and emerging technologies, the application of data diversity plays a crucial role in enhancing the performance and fairness of systems across various contexts. Data diversity encompasses a wide array of dimensions including demographic, contextual, temporal, and domain-specific variations. Each of these dimensions contributes uniquely to the robustness and inclusivity of AI models.

In healthcare, the integration of diverse medical records significantly improves diagnostic accuracy and treatment plans across different patient populations. For instance, demographic diversity ensures that AI models are trained on data representing varied age groups, ethnicities, and genders, which is critical in developing equitable

33

healthcare solutions. Contextual diversity, which involves data from different environments and cultural settings, further refines these models to be sensitive to local nuances and patient needs.

The realm of autonomous systems, such as self-driving cars, benefits immensely from data diversity. These systems require robust training data that captures a multitude of environmental conditions, from urban to rural settings, and varying weather patterns. By incorporating contextual and temporal diversity, autonomous systems can better predict and adapt to unforeseen circumstances, thereby enhancing safety and reliability.

In natural language processing (NLP), data diversity is indispensable for developing models that understand and generate human language effectively. Multilingual and culturally diverse datasets are essential for creating language models that can serve global audiences. This diversity allows AI to process and interpret languages with different syntactic and semantic structures, promoting inclusivity and accessibility in digital communication.

Retail and marketing sectors leverage data diversity to tailor personalized experiences for consumers worldwide. By analyzing diverse consumer data, businesses can better understand purchasing behaviors and preferences across different demographics and regions. This not only boosts customer satisfaction but also drives innovation in product development and marketing strategies.

Despite its advantages, achieving data diversity poses several challenges. Bias in data collection often leads to the underrepresentation of certain groups, while the availability of diverse datasets can be limited, particularly in specialized domains. Moreover, the cost and complexity of gathering diverse data, coupled with regulatory and privacy constraints, can hinder efforts to enhance data diversity.

To address these challenges, strategies such as inclusive data sourcing and the use of synthetic data are employed. Synthetic data generation, through advanced generative models, allows for the simulation of diverse scenarios, providing a viable alternative when real-world data is scarce. Additionally, cross-domain collaboration and federated learning enable organizations to access varied datasets while maintaining data privacy and security.

Ultimately, data diversity is foundational to the development of AI systems that are not only technically proficient but also ethically sound and socially responsible. By fostering inclusivity and fairness, data diversity ensures that AI technologies can effectively meet the diverse needs of global populations, paving the way for more equitable and impactful technological advancements.

Challenges and Solutions

In the realm of artificial intelligence and emerging technologies, data diversity presents both significant challenges and potential solutions.

As AI systems are increasingly integrated into various aspects of society, ensuring that these systems are built on diverse datasets becomes crucial. However, achieving this diversity is fraught with obstacles that need to be carefully navigated.

One of the primary challenges in attaining data diversity is the inherent bias in data collection processes. Often, datasets are skewed due to underrepresentation of certain demographics or scenarios. This can stem from systemic issues or limited access to comprehensive data sources, leading to AI models that do not perform equitably across different populations. Such biases can perpetuate inequalities and result in AI systems that are less effective or even harmful.

Another significant hurdle is the availability of diverse, high-quality datasets, especially in specialized domains. Data scarcity can impede the development of robust AI models, as limited data diversity hinders the ability to generalize across varying real-world situations. Furthermore, the cost and complexity associated with gathering and managing diverse datasets can be prohibitive. The process requires substantial resources, including time, expertise, and financial investment, which may not always be feasible for all organizations.

Regulatory and privacy constraints add another layer of complexity. Legal and ethical considerations regarding the use of sensitive or protected data must be addressed to ensure compliance with data protection regulations such as GDPR and CCPA. These constraints can limit the accessibility of necessary data, thus impacting the diversity of datasets available for AI training and development.

Despite these challenges, several strategies can be employed to promote data diversity effectively. Inclusive data sourcing involves actively seeking out data from underrepresented groups and contexts, thereby enriching the datasets used for AI model training. Additionally, the use of synthetic data, generated by advanced models to simulate diverse scenarios, can be a valuable tool when real-world data is insufficient.

Collaboration across domains and regions is another effective strategy. By partnering with organizations from various industries and geographical locations, access to a broader range of datasets can be achieved. This cross-domain collaboration not only enhances data diversity but also fosters innovation by bringing together different perspectives and expertise.

Regular bias auditing and the implementation of specialized metrics are crucial in evaluating datasets for gaps and biases. These tools enable organizations to identify and address potential biases, ensuring that AI systems are fair and equitable. Moreover, federated learning offers a promising approach by leveraging decentralized data sources while maintaining privacy and security, thus facilitating data diversity without compromising individual privacy.

In summary, while challenges in achieving data diversity are substantial, the solutions are within reach through deliberate and collaborative efforts. By addressing biases, enhancing data availability, and navigating regulatory constraints, the development of inclusive and effective AI systems can be realized. These efforts not only improve the performance and fairness of AI models but also contribute to the broader goal of creating technology that serves all sectors of society equitably.

Future Trends

As we navigate the rapidly evolving landscape of artificial intelligence and emerging technologies, it becomes increasingly clear that data diversity will play a pivotal role in shaping future trends. The importance of data diversity cannot be overstated, as it ensures that AI systems are inclusive, fair, and effective across a wide range of populations and scenarios. This involves embracing a variety of data types, including demographic, contextual, temporal, and domain-specific diversity.

In the future, we can expect AI systems to be trained on datasets that are far more comprehensive and representative of the world's complexity. This shift is driven by the need to minimize bias and improve the robustness of AI applications in real-world settings. As AI becomes more integrated into everyday life, the demand for systems that can understand and adapt to diverse inputs will grow.

One of the significant trends we anticipate is the increased use of synthetic data to fill gaps where real-world data is scarce or difficult to obtain. Synthetic data can simulate a wide range of scenarios and demographics, providing a valuable resource for training AI models. This approach not only enhances data diversity but also helps to overcome privacy and regulatory challenges associated with using real data.

Another trend is the rise of cross-domain collaboration. Organizations from different sectors and regions will increasingly partner to share data and insights, creating a richer tapestry of information for AI systems to learn from. This collaborative approach will spur innovation and lead to the development of more sophisticated AI applications that can tackle complex global challenges.

Federated learning is also set to become a cornerstone of future AI development. By leveraging decentralized data sources, federated learning allows models to be trained on diverse datasets while maintaining privacy and security. This method not only enhances data diversity but also ensures compliance with strict data protection regulations.

As AI systems evolve, there will be a greater emphasis on bias auditing and the use of metrics to evaluate datasets for gaps and imbalances. Regular assessments will be crucial to maintaining the integrity and fairness of AI applications, ensuring they serve all communities equitably.

In terms of applications, data diversity will have profound implications across various domains. In healthcare, for instance, diverse medical records will lead to more accurate diagnostics and treatments tailored to individual patient needs. In autonomous systems, such as self-driving cars, a wide array of environmental data will enhance safety and adaptability in different conditions.

The field of natural language processing (NLP) will also benefit significantly from data diversity. As language models are exposed to multilingual and culturally varied data, they will become more proficient in understanding and generating human-like text across different languages and dialects. This will facilitate better communication and interaction in a globalized world.

Retail and marketing sectors will leverage diverse consumer data to deliver personalized experiences to a global audience, tailoring products and services to meet the unique preferences of different customer segments.

Overall, the future of AI and emerging technologies is inextricably linked to the pursuit of data diversity. By embracing this diversity, we can build AI systems that are not only more effective and resilient but also more ethical and aligned with the diverse needs of society.

Chapter 4: Temporal Diversity
Data Over Time

The evolution of data over time plays a pivotal role in shaping the landscape of artificial intelligence and emerging technologies. As technology progresses, the nature of data collection, analysis, and application undergoes significant transformation. Understanding these temporal dynamics is crucial for developing AI systems that are both robust and adaptable.

Data collected over varying time periods captures the nuances of trends and seasonality, which are essential for accurate predictions and decision-making. For instance, temporal datasets allow AI models to account for cyclical patterns in consumer behavior, economic fluctuations, and even environmental changes. This capability is particularly important in applications such as financial forecasting, climate modeling, and trend analysis in social media.

The historical context of data provides insights into the evolution of societal norms and technological advancements. By analyzing data from different eras, researchers can identify shifts in public opinion, technological adoption rates, and the emergence of new industries. This temporal perspective not only aids in understanding past trends but also in anticipating future developments, enabling proactive strategies in business and policy-making.

Moreover, temporal data diversity enhances the generalization ability of AI models. By training models on datasets that span multiple time periods, developers can ensure that these systems remain effective even as conditions change. This is particularly relevant in industries where rapid innovation or regulatory changes frequently alter the landscape, such as healthcare, finance, and technology.

However, leveraging temporal data diversity presents its own set of challenges. One major issue is the alignment of datasets collected at different times, which may vary in terms of format, quality, and context. Ensuring consistency and compatibility across temporal datasets requires sophisticated data integration techniques and a deep understanding of the domain-specific factors that influence data collection.

Additionally, the availability of historical data can be limited by factors such as data degradation, loss, or changes in data collection methods over time. These limitations necessitate innovative approaches to data preservation and restoration, as well as the use of synthetic data generation to fill gaps where historical data is unavailable.

Ethical considerations also arise when dealing with temporal data, particularly concerning privacy and consent. As data is collected over time, the context in which it was gathered may change, leading to potential issues with data ownership and usage rights. Ensuring compliance with evolving data protection regulations, such as GDPR and CCPA, is essential to maintain ethical standards and protect individual privacy.

In summary, the temporal dimension of data is a critical component in the development of AI and emerging technologies. By embracing data diversity over time, we can create AI systems that are not only more accurate and reliable but also more reflective of the dynamic world in which they operate. This approach fosters innovation and resilience, enabling AI technologies to better serve the diverse and ever-changing needs of society.

Trends and Seasonality

In the realm of artificial intelligence and emerging technologies, understanding trends and seasonality is pivotal for harnessing the full potential of data diversity. Trends refer to the long-term movement or direction in which data points evolve over time, whereas seasonality denotes the periodic fluctuations or patterns that occur at regular intervals within a dataset. These phenomena are crucial for developing AI systems that are both adaptive and predictive, allowing them to respond to changing conditions and cyclic behaviors effectively.

Data diversity plays a significant role in capturing trends and seasonality. By incorporating a wide range of data types and sources, AI models can be trained to recognize and adapt to diverse temporal patterns. Temporal diversity, in particular, involves collecting data over different time periods to ensure that both trends and seasonal variations are well represented. This approach not only enhances the robustness of AI models but also mitigates the risk of bias that might arise from over-reliance on data from a specific time frame or context.

Incorporating trends and seasonality into AI systems requires meticulous data collection and analysis. For instance, in the field of predictive analytics, understanding seasonal demand patterns can significantly improve inventory management and resource allocation. By analyzing historical data, AI systems can forecast future trends and adjust strategies accordingly, ensuring that businesses remain competitive and responsive to market changes.

Moreover, in climate science, recognizing seasonal variations is essential for accurate weather forecasting and climate modeling. AI models that leverage data diversity to capture these patterns can provide more reliable predictions, aiding in disaster preparedness and resource management. Similarly, in healthcare, identifying trends in patient data, such as seasonal outbreaks of illnesses, can enhance preventive measures and optimize healthcare delivery.

The challenges of integrating trends and seasonality into AI systems are nontrivial. Data must be meticulously curated to ensure it reflects the full spectrum of temporal variations. This includes addressing potential biases in data collection processes and ensuring that datasets are sufficiently large and diverse to capture the nuances of trends and seasonality. Additionally, AI models must be equipped with sophisticated algorithms capable of discerning these patterns amidst noise and variability in the data.

One effective strategy is the use of machine learning techniques such as time series analysis, which focuses on analyzing data points collected or recorded at specific time intervals. These techniques enable the detection of underlying trends and seasonal patterns, facilitating more accurate forecasting and decision-making. Furthermore, advancements in deep learning have introduced neural networks capable of modeling complex temporal dependencies, further enhancing the ability of AI systems to learn from and adapt to dynamic environments.

In summary, the integration of trends and seasonality into AI and emerging technologies is a critical component of leveraging data diversity. By embracing a comprehensive approach to data collection and analysis, AI systems can achieve greater accuracy, adaptability, and fairness, ultimately leading to more innovative and effective solutions across various domains. As the landscape of AI continues to evolve, the importance of understanding and utilizing trends and seasonality will only grow, underscoring the need for continued research and development in this area.

Temporal Bias

Temporal bias in AI systems arises when data used for training, validating, or testing models does not adequately represent the temporal variations and trends inherent in the real world. This form of bias can lead to models that are overly fitted to specific time periods, resulting in poor performance when applied to data from different temporal contexts. Temporal bias can manifest in various ways, such as seasonality, trends, and cyclical patterns that are not captured in the data.

One of the primary challenges in addressing temporal bias is the dynamic nature of data. Unlike static datasets, temporal data is constantly evolving, influenced by factors such as technological advancements, socio-economic changes, and cultural shifts. This necessitates a continuous updating of datasets to ensure they remain representative of current conditions. Failure to do so can lead to models that are outdated or irrelevant, as they may base their predictions on patterns that no longer hold true.

To mitigate temporal bias, it is crucial to incorporate data from various time periods during the model development process. This involves collecting historical data that captures past trends and seasonality, as well as real-time data that reflects current conditions. By doing so, models can be trained to recognize and adapt to temporal variations, improving their robustness and generalization capabilities. Additionally, techniques such as time series analysis and temporal cross-validation can be employed to evaluate model performance across different time frames, ensuring they are not overly reliant on data from a specific period.

Moreover, understanding the temporal context of data is essential for interpreting model outputs and making informed decisions. For instance, a predictive model in finance might leverage historical stock prices to forecast future market movements. However, if the model does not account for temporal factors like economic recessions or policy changes, its predictions may be inaccurate or misleading. Therefore, integrating temporal awareness into AI systems is vital for enhancing their reliability and effectiveness.

Another aspect of temporal bias is its impact on fairness and equity. Temporal changes can affect different demographic groups in varying ways, leading to disparities in how AI systems perform across populations. For example, a healthcare model trained on data from a particular time frame might not account for recent medical discoveries or shifts in demographic health trends, potentially disadvantaging certain groups. Ensuring temporal diversity in data can help address these issues by providing a more comprehensive view of how different populations are affected over time.

In the realm of emerging technologies, addressing temporal bias is particularly important as these systems are often deployed in rapidly changing environments. Autonomous vehicles, for instance, must adapt to varying traffic patterns and weather conditions, which can fluctuate significantly over time. Similarly, natural language processing models must keep pace with evolving language use and cultural references to remain relevant.

Ultimately, combating temporal bias requires a proactive approach to data collection and model evaluation, emphasizing the importance of staying attuned to temporal dynamics. By prioritizing temporal diversity, AI systems can achieve greater accuracy, fairness, and adaptability, thereby enhancing their applicability and trustworthiness in diverse real-world scenarios.

Case Studies

In the exploration of data diversity within AI and emerging technologies, case studies offer invaluable insights into the practical applications and challenges faced in real-world scenarios. These case studies illuminate the pathways through which data diversity can be leveraged to enhance AI systems' performance, fairness, and robustness across various domains.

One notable example is in the healthcare sector, where data diversity plays a crucial role in improving diagnostic accuracy. By incorporating diverse datasets that include a wide range of demographic and contextual variables, AI models can better predict and diagnose medical conditions across different populations. This approach not only reduces bias but also ensures that healthcare solutions are more inclusive and equitable.

In the realm of autonomous systems, such as self-driving cars, diverse environmental data is essential for enhancing safety and adaptability. Case studies have shown that training models with data from varied geographical locations, weather conditions, and traffic scenarios enables these systems to perform more reliably in unexpected situations. This diversity in data allows autonomous systems to generalize better and handle edge cases that would otherwise pose significant risks.

Natural Language Processing (NLP) also greatly benefits from data diversity. Multilingual and culturally varied datasets enrich language models, enabling them to understand and generate text that is contextually and culturally relevant. This is particularly important in global applications where language models must cater to users from diverse linguistic backgrounds. Case studies in this field demonstrate how diverse data sets improve language translation accuracy and the overall user experience.

In retail and marketing, diverse consumer data is instrumental in creating personalized experiences for a global audience. By analyzing data that reflects a wide array of consumer preferences, behaviors, and cultural nuances, companies can tailor their marketing strategies to resonate with different demographic groups. This not only enhances customer satisfaction but also drives business growth by tapping into previously underserved markets.

Despite the evident benefits, achieving data diversity is not without its challenges. Case studies often highlight issues such as bias in data collection, where certain groups or scenarios are underrepresented due to systemic issues or limited access to data sources. Additionally, the availability of diverse, high-quality datasets in specialized domains can be scarce, posing significant barriers to data diversity.

Moreover, the cost and complexity of gathering and managing diverse datasets can be resource-intensive. Organizations must navigate regulatory and privacy constraints that govern access to sensitive or protected data. These challenges necessitate innovative strategies, such as synthetic data generation and federated learning, to simulate diverse scenarios while maintaining privacy and security.

Through these case studies, the importance of cross-domain collaboration becomes evident. Partnering with organizations across industries and regions can facilitate access to varied datasets, promoting broader data diversity. Regular bias auditing and the implementation of metrics to evaluate datasets for gaps and biases are also crucial in ensuring that AI systems are fair and effective.

In summary, case studies on data diversity in AI and emerging technologies underscore the significance of inclusive data practices. By learning from these real-world examples, stakeholders can better address the challenges and harness the full potential of diverse datasets to create AI systems that are robust, ethical, and impactful across diverse global needs.

Implications for AI

The integration of data diversity into AI systems holds profound implications for the field, influencing how these technologies are developed, deployed, and perceived across various domains. As AI continues to permeate numerous aspects of life, ensuring that these systems are trained on diverse datasets becomes critical to their success and acceptance.

One of the primary implications is the enhancement of AI model robustness. By incorporating diverse datasets, AI systems can generalize better across different environments, cultures, and demographics. This diversity allows these systems to perform reliably in a wide range of scenarios, thus increasing their utility and effectiveness. For instance, in natural language processing, models trained on multilingual and culturally varied data can more accurately interpret and generate language across different contexts, thereby improving communication technologies globally.

Moreover, data diversity plays a crucial role in mitigating biases inherent in AI models. Bias in AI can lead to unfair treatment of individuals based on race, gender, or other demographic factors. By ensuring that training datasets include a wide range of perspectives and experiences, AI developers can reduce the risk of perpetuating these biases. This not only leads to fairer outcomes but also builds trust in AI systems among users and stakeholders.

The pursuit of data diversity also encourages innovation within the AI field. When researchers and developers have access to a broad spectrum of data, they can uncover new patterns and insights that might not be evident in more homogenous datasets. This can lead to the development of novel AI applications and solutions that address previously unmet needs or improve existing processes.

Additionally, the emphasis on data diversity necessitates the adoption of new data management and processing techniques. Techniques such as federated learning allow AI systems to learn from decentralized data sources while maintaining privacy and security, addressing some of the ethical and regulatory challenges associated with accessing diverse datasets. Synthetic data generation is another method that can supplement real-world data, providing additional diversity where gaps exist.

However, achieving data diversity is not without its challenges. Collecting and maintaining diverse datasets can be resource-intensive, requiring significant investments in time and technology. Moreover, ethical considerations such as privacy and consent must be carefully navigated to ensure that data diversity efforts do not infringe on individual rights or societal norms.

Ultimately, the implications of data diversity for AI are expansive, touching on technical, ethical, and societal dimensions. It is a foundational element in the development of AI systems that are not only effective and innovative but also equitable and trustworthy. As the field progresses, ongoing efforts to promote data diversity will be essential in shaping AI technologies that reflect and respect the diverse world they aim to serve.

Chapter 5: Domain-Specific Diversity
Healthcare Data

In the realm of data diversity, healthcare data plays a pivotal role in advancing artificial intelligence (AI) and emerging technologies. The diversity in healthcare data is not just a reflection of the varied patient demographics but also encompasses the multitude of settings, conditions, and treatments encountered across the healthcare spectrum. This diversity is critical for developing AI systems that are robust, equitable, and capable of delivering accurate and personalized healthcare solutions.

Healthcare data is characterized by its vast and varied nature, encompassing patient records, diagnostic images, genomic sequences, and real-time monitoring data from wearable devices. Each of these data types contributes to a comprehensive understanding of patient health and medical conditions. The inclusion of diverse healthcare data in AI models ensures that these systems can cater to a wide range of populations, addressing the unique health challenges faced by different demographic groups. For instance, incorporating data from various ethnic groups helps in identifying disease patterns that are specific to those communities, thereby enabling the development of targeted interventions and treatments.

The integration of diverse healthcare data into AI systems also enhances diagnostic accuracy. AI models trained on a wide array of medical images, for example, are more adept at identifying anomalies across different patient groups. This is particularly important in radiology, where the subtle differences in imaging across diverse populations can impact the diagnosis and treatment plans. Moreover, the use of genomic data from a diverse population allows for the discovery of genetic markers that are significant in certain ethnic groups but may be overlooked in homogenous datasets.

However, achieving diversity in healthcare data is fraught with challenges. One of the primary hurdles is the underrepresentation of certain groups in medical datasets. This can result from systemic biases in data collection practices, limited access to healthcare services, or socioeconomic barriers that prevent certain populations from being adequately represented. Addressing these gaps requires concerted efforts to collect data from underrepresented groups and ensure that AI systems do not perpetuate existing healthcare disparities.

Furthermore, the sensitive nature of healthcare data poses significant privacy and ethical concerns. Ensuring compliance with regulations such as the General Data Protection Regulation (GDPR) and the Health Insurance Portability and Accountability Act (HIPAA) is crucial in maintaining patient confidentiality while promoting data diversity. Innovative approaches such as federated learning, which allows AI models to be trained on decentralized data sources without compromising privacy, offer promising solutions to these challenges.

In summary, the diversity of healthcare data is essential for the development of AI systems that are inclusive and equitable. By addressing the challenges of data diversity, the healthcare industry can harness the full potential of AI and emerging technologies to improve patient outcomes, reduce health disparities, and deliver personalized care. The ongoing efforts to diversify healthcare data will not only enhance the capabilities of AI systems but also pave the way for a more inclusive and effective healthcare ecosystem.

Manufacturing Sensors

In the realm of modern manufacturing, sensors play a pivotal role in digitizing and optimizing production processes. These sensors are integral to the development and implementation of smart manufacturing systems, which rely on real-time data collection and analysis to improve efficiency and productivity. By embedding sensors within machinery and production lines, manufacturers can monitor various parameters such as temperature, pressure, vibration, and humidity. This data is then used to predict equipment failures, optimize maintenance schedules, and enhance product quality.

The integration of sensors in manufacturing is not merely about collecting data but about transforming that data into actionable insights. Advanced sensors are equipped with capabilities to detect anomalies and provide alerts before a malfunction occurs. This predictive maintenance approach not only minimizes downtime but also extends the lifespan of equipment, leading to significant cost savings. Moreover, the data collected from these sensors can be fed into machine learning algorithms to further refine operational processes and product designs.

Another crucial aspect of manufacturing sensors is their role in ensuring quality control. By continuously monitoring production parameters, sensors help maintain consistency and adherence to quality standards. This real-time quality assurance is essential in industries where precision is paramount, such as in the automotive or aerospace sectors. Sensors can detect even the slightest deviations from the set parameters, allowing for immediate corrective actions, thereby reducing waste and rework.

The diversity of sensors available for manufacturing applications is vast, ranging from simple temperature sensors to complex multi-sensor systems that can capture a wide array of data points. This diversity enables manufacturers to tailor their sensor networks to meet specific production needs and challenges. For instance, in a high-speed production environment, optical sensors might be used to ensure that all components are correctly aligned and assembled.

However, the deployment of sensors in manufacturing also presents challenges. One significant issue is the integration of sensor data with existing IT infrastructure. Ensuring seamless communication between sensors and central data systems is crucial for maximizing the value of collected data. Additionally, the sheer volume of data generated by sensors can be overwhelming, requiring robust data management and analysis tools to extract meaningful insights.

Moreover, as manufacturing sensors become increasingly sophisticated, concerns about data security and privacy have emerged. Protecting sensitive production data from cyber threats is a top priority for manufacturers, necessitating the implementation of stringent security protocols and measures.

In conclusion, the role of sensors in manufacturing is indispensable for driving the industry towards greater efficiency and innovation. By harnessing the power of sensor technology, manufacturers can achieve higher levels of precision and control, ultimately leading to improved product quality and operational excellence. As technology continues to advance, the capabilities and applications of manufacturing sensors will undoubtedly expand, offering new opportunities for growth and development in the manufacturing sector.

Educational Datasets

In the realm of artificial intelligence and emerging technologies, the utilization of educational datasets plays a pivotal role in shaping the capabilities and fairness of AI systems. These datasets, which are specifically curated from educational environments, encompass a wide range of data points, including student demographics, learning outcomes, and pedagogical methods. The diversity inherent in educational datasets is critical for developing AI models that are not only robust but also equitable and inclusive.

Educational datasets provide a unique blend of demographic and contextual diversity, reflecting the varied backgrounds and learning environments of students globally. This diversity is essential for training AI models to recognize and adapt to different educational needs and contexts. For instance, datasets that include information from urban and rural schools, or those with varied levels of resource availability, help in creating AI systems that can cater to a broad spectrum of educational settings.

The integration of educational datasets into AI systems also addresses the issue of bias, which is a significant challenge in AI development. By ensuring that the datasets are representative of diverse student populations, AI developers can mitigate biases that might otherwise lead to inequitable learning outcomes. For example, if a dataset predominantly consists of data from well-funded schools, the AI model might not perform well in under-resourced settings. Therefore, incorporating a wide array of data from different educational contexts ensures that the AI systems are fair and effective for all students.

Moreover, educational datasets contribute to the innovation in AI-driven educational tools and platforms. With access to diverse data, AI can be used to develop personalized learning experiences that cater to the individual needs of students. This personalization is crucial in addressing the varying paces at which students learn and the different challenges they face. AI systems can analyze patterns in educational data to provide tailored recommendations, thus enhancing the learning experience and outcomes for students.

The challenges associated with using educational datasets include ensuring data privacy and security, as educational data often contains sensitive information about students. Compliance with regulations such as GDPR and CCPA is necessary to protect student privacy while utilizing these datasets for AI development. Additionally, there is a need for collaboration between educational institutions and AI developers to ensure that the datasets are used ethically and responsibly.

In summary, educational datasets are indispensable for advancing AI in education. They provide the necessary diversity and depth required to build AI systems that are adaptable, fair, and innovative. By leveraging these datasets, AI can transform educational experiences, making them more inclusive and effective for students worldwide. The ongoing collaboration between educators, policymakers, and AI developers will be crucial in harnessing the full potential of educational datasets, ensuring that AI continues to support and enhance educational outcomes for future generations.

Challenges in Different Domains

In the realm of artificial intelligence and emerging technologies, data diversity poses significant challenges across various domains. These challenges arise from the inherent complexity and unique requirements of each sector, which demand tailored approaches to ensure that AI systems are robust, fair, and effective.

In healthcare, for instance, the diversity of medical data is crucial for developing accurate diagnostic tools and treatment plans. However, achieving this diversity is hampered by privacy concerns and regulatory constraints that limit access to comprehensive datasets. The heterogeneity in patient demographics, medical histories, and treatment outcomes necessitates diverse data sourcing to prevent biases that could lead to suboptimal care for underrepresented groups.

The automotive industry, particularly in the development of autonomous systems, faces its own set of challenges. The vast array of environmental conditions, including weather variations, urban versus rural settings, and different traffic laws, requires an extensive collection of diverse data to train reliable AI models. The scarcity of such data, along with the cost and complexity of acquiring it, can hinder the development of systems that are truly safe and adaptable to all driving scenarios.

In the field of natural language processing (NLP), linguistic diversity is a major hurdle. AI models must be trained on data that encompasses a wide range of languages and dialects to ensure accurate and culturally sensitive interactions. However, many languages, especially those spoken by smaller populations, are underrepresented in existing datasets. This lack of linguistic diversity can lead to AI systems that are biased towards more widely spoken languages, thus marginalizing speakers of less common tongues.

Retail and marketing sectors also grapple with the challenge of data diversity. To deliver personalized experiences to a global customer base, AI models need access to diverse consumer data that reflects varying cultural preferences and purchasing behaviors. The challenge lies in the integration of this data from multiple sources while maintaining compliance with privacy regulations like GDPR and CCPA.

Moreover, across all these domains, the challenge of bias in data collection is prevalent. Systemic issues often lead to the underrepresentation of certain groups, which can perpetuate biases in AI systems. Addressing these biases requires deliberate efforts to include diverse datasets and implement bias auditing procedures.

To overcome these challenges, strategies such as synthetic data generation and cross-domain collaboration are being explored. Synthetic data can simulate diverse scenarios where real-world data is limited, while partnerships across industries can provide access to varied datasets. Additionally, federated learning offers a way to leverage decentralized data sources while maintaining privacy and security.

Ultimately, the pursuit of data diversity in AI and emerging technologies is a multifaceted endeavor. It involves not only technical solutions but also ethical and governance considerations to ensure that AI systems are inclusive and equitable. By addressing these challenges, we can build AI systems that better serve the diverse needs of the global population.

Opportunities for Innovation

In the rapidly evolving landscape of artificial intelligence and emerging technologies, there lies a substantial opportunity for innovation driven by data diversity. The inclusion of diverse datasets not only enriches AI models but also propels innovation in ways previously unimagined. This diversity encompasses a wide spectrum of data types including demographic, contextual, temporal, and domain-specific variations, each contributing uniquely to the development of robust AI systems.

Demographic diversity, for instance, ensures that AI systems can cater to a broader audience by encompassing a range of ages, genders, ethnicities, and socioeconomic backgrounds. This inclusivity is crucial in creating AI solutions that are fair and equitable, thereby opening avenues for innovations that address the needs of underrepresented groups. By considering a diverse demographic, new product designs and services can emerge, tailored to meet the specific needs of various communities, thus expanding market reach and enhancing user satisfaction.

Contextual diversity further enhances innovation by incorporating data from varied environments and cultural contexts. This diversity enables the creation of AI systems that are adaptable and responsive to different scenarios and cultural nuances. For example, in the field of autonomous systems, incorporating data from both urban and rural environments ensures that the systems can operate safely and effectively in diverse settings. Such adaptability is crucial in emerging technologies where context-specific solutions can lead to groundbreaking advancements.

Temporal diversity, which involves data collected over different time periods, allows AI systems to capture trends and seasonal variations, thus providing insights that are vital for long-term strategic planning and innovation. This approach can lead to the development of AI models that not only understand current patterns but also predict future trends, offering a competitive edge in industries such as finance and retail.

Domain-specific diversity brings about innovation by leveraging data unique to particular industries. In healthcare, for example, diverse datasets can improve diagnostic accuracy and treatment efficacy across different populations. This not only enhances patient outcomes but also stimulates innovation in medical research and healthcare delivery systems.

The challenges associated with achieving data diversity, such as bias in data collection and privacy concerns, should not deter the pursuit of innovation. Instead, they present opportunities to develop new methodologies and technologies that address these issues. Techniques such as synthetic data generation and federated learning are examples of innovative solutions that help overcome these challenges while maintaining data diversity.

By fostering collaboration across domains and regions, organizations can access a wider array of datasets, leading to richer and more innovative AI applications. This cross-domain collaboration is a catalyst for innovation, as it combines expertise and perspectives from different fields, leading to novel insights and breakthroughs.

In conclusion, embracing data diversity is not merely a matter of ethical responsibility but a strategic imperative for driving innovation in AI and emerging technologies. By leveraging diverse datasets, organizations can develop AI systems that are more inclusive, equitable, and capable of addressing complex global challenges. This approach not only enhances the capabilities of AI technologies but also paves the way for continuous innovation and improvement in various sectors.

Chapter 6: Bias in Data Collection
Systemic Issues

In the realm of artificial intelligence and emerging technologies, systemic issues present significant challenges to achieving data diversity. These challenges are rooted in the complex interplay of social, economic, and technical factors that influence the collection, representation, and utilization of data across various domains. At the heart of these systemic issues is the inherent bias that can arise from data collection processes. Often, data sets lack representation of certain groups or scenarios due to historical biases, limited access to diverse data sources, or intentional exclusions. This underrepresentation can lead to AI systems that are not only biased but also ineffective when deployed in diverse real-world contexts.

Moreover, the availability of diverse, high-quality datasets is a persistent challenge. In many specialized fields, such as healthcare or autonomous systems, there is a scarcity of data that adequately captures the diversity required to develop robust AI models. This scarcity is often exacerbated by the high costs and complexities associated with gathering and managing such datasets. For instance, collecting comprehensive demographic or contextual data may require significant resources, both in terms of time and financial investment, which may not be feasible for all organizations.

Regulatory and privacy constraints further complicate the landscape, as legal and ethical considerations must be navigated when accessing and utilizing sensitive or protected data. Regulations such as the General Data Protection Regulation (GDPR) and the California Consumer Privacy Act (CCPA) impose stringent requirements on data collection and processing, which can limit the ability to gather diverse datasets. These constraints necessitate a careful balance between innovation and compliance, ensuring that data diversity efforts do not infringe upon individual rights or societal norms.

To address these systemic issues, several strategies have been proposed. Inclusive data sourcing is one such approach, which involves actively seeking data from underrepresented groups and contexts. This can help to fill the gaps in existing datasets and ensure that AI models are trained on a more comprehensive representation of the population. Additionally, the use of synthetic data, generated through advanced algorithms and simulations, offers a promising avenue for simulating diverse scenarios where real-world data is limited.

Cross-domain collaboration also plays a crucial role in overcoming systemic barriers to data diversity. By partnering with organizations across different industries and regions, stakeholders can access a wider array of datasets, fostering a more holistic approach to AI development. Furthermore, implementing bias auditing and metrics can aid in regularly evaluating datasets for gaps and biases, using specialized tools and frameworks to ensure ongoing improvement.

Lastly, federated learning emerges as a novel solution, allowing for the utilization of decentralized data sources while maintaining privacy and security. This approach enables the training of AI models on diverse datasets without the need to centralize sensitive data, thus addressing both diversity and privacy concerns simultaneously. By tackling these systemic issues, the field of AI can advance towards creating more inclusive and equitable technologies that reflect the rich diversity of human experiences.

Underrepresentation

The phenomenon of underrepresentation within data sets used for artificial intelligence (AI) and emerging technologies is an intricate issue with far-reaching implications. The lack of adequate representation of diverse groups in data collection can lead to skewed AI models that fail to serve all segments of society equitably. This issue is deeply rooted in systemic biases and limited access to comprehensive data sources, which often exclude marginalized communities and minority groups. In AI development, the datasets are predominantly sourced from regions and demographics that are easily accessible or economically viable, leading to a significant imbalance. This imbalance manifests in AI systems that do not accurately reflect or address the needs of global populations, particularly those from underrepresented backgrounds.

The consequences of such underrepresentation are manifold. AI systems trained on biased data may produce outputs that perpetuate existing inequalities, thereby reinforcing stereotypes and discrimination. This is particularly evident in facial recognition technologies, where models often perform poorly on individuals with darker skin tones due to the lack of diverse training data. Similarly, natural language processing tools may misunderstand or misrepresent dialects and languages spoken by minority groups, leading to ineffective communication and service delivery.

To address these challenges, it is crucial to implement strategies that promote data diversity and inclusivity. One approach is to actively source data from a wider range of demographics and contexts. This involves reaching out to underrepresented communities and involving them in the data collection process. Additionally, leveraging synthetic data generation can help simulate diverse scenarios and fill gaps where real-world data is scarce. This approach, however, must be handled with care to ensure that the synthetic data accurately reflects the complexities of real-world diversity.

Collaboration across industries and regions is another effective strategy to enhance data diversity. By partnering with organizations from various sectors, AI developers can access a broader spectrum of datasets that encompass different cultural, environmental, and socio-economic backgrounds. Moreover, regular bias auditing and the application of fairness metrics are essential to identify and mitigate gaps in datasets. These measures help ensure that AI systems are not only diverse but also fair and just in their operations.

Federated learning presents a promising avenue for maintaining diversity while upholding privacy standards. This method allows AI models to be trained on decentralized data sources, which can include sensitive or protected data from various locales, without compromising individual privacy. By enabling data to remain within its local context, federated learning minimizes the risk of data breaches and respects regulatory constraints.

Ultimately, addressing underrepresentation in AI and emerging technologies requires a concerted effort from all stakeholders involved. It necessitates a paradigm shift towards ethical data practices and a commitment to inclusivity at every stage of AI development. By embracing diversity in data, we can pave the way for more equitable and effective AI systems that truly reflect the global tapestry of human experience.

Impact on AI Models

Data diversity plays a crucial role in shaping the capabilities and limitations of AI models. As AI continues to permeate various sectors, the demand for models that can function effectively across diverse scenarios and populations has intensified. The diversity in data refers to the variety and richness in the datasets used for training, validating, and testing AI systems. This includes variations in demographics, languages, cultural contexts, environments, and specific scenarios. Such diversity ensures that AI models are inclusive, fair, and effective, minimizing biases and enhancing robustness.

AI models trained on diverse datasets are better equipped to generalize across different real-world situations. For instance, demographic diversity ensures that models do not favor or disadvantage certain age groups, genders, ethnicities, or socioeconomic classes. Contextual diversity, on the other hand, prepares models to handle variations in environments, such as urban versus rural settings, and different cultural contexts, enhancing their adaptability and accuracy in various use cases.

Temporal diversity is another critical aspect, as it involves collecting data over different time periods to capture trends and seasonality. This is particularly important for applications that are sensitive to time-related changes, such as financial forecasting or climate modeling. Domain-specific diversity, meanwhile, enriches AI models with industry-specific data, which is crucial for fields like healthcare, where diverse medical records can improve diagnostic accuracy and treatment efficacy across populations.

Despite the clear benefits, achieving data diversity poses several challenges. Bias in data collection often results in the underrepresentation of certain groups or scenarios, primarily due to systemic issues or limited access to diverse data sources. Additionally, the availability of diverse, high-quality datasets is often scarce, especially in specialized domains. The cost and complexity of gathering and managing such datasets can be resource-intensive, and there are also regulatory and privacy constraints that need to be navigated carefully.

To address these challenges, various strategies can be employed. Inclusive data sourcing actively seeks data from underrepresented groups and contexts. Synthetic data generation, using generative models, can simulate diverse scenarios when real-world data is unavailable. Cross-domain collaboration with organizations across industries and regions can open up access to varied datasets. Moreover, bias auditing and metrics help in regularly evaluating datasets for gaps and biases, while federated learning leverages decentralized data sources while maintaining privacy and security.

The impact of data diversity on AI models extends to emerging technologies as well. In healthcare, diverse data can enhance diagnostic tools, making them more accurate and reliable across different populations. For autonomous systems, environmental diversity is crucial for ensuring safety and adaptability in varying conditions. In natural language processing, multilingual and culturally varied data are essential for improving language models, enabling them to understand and process information more effectively across different languages and cultural nuances. Lastly, in retail and marketing, diverse consumer data allows for the creation of personalized experiences for a global audience, enhancing customer satisfaction and engagement.

Overall, data diversity is foundational for developing AI systems that are robust, ethical, and capable of serving diverse global needs effectively.

Solutions and Approaches

In the realm of artificial intelligence and emerging technologies, addressing data diversity is pivotal for enhancing model performance and ensuring equitable outcomes. Solutions and approaches to achieving data diversity encompass several strategic actions that target the core challenges associated with creating inclusive datasets.

One fundamental approach is the deliberate sourcing of inclusive data. This involves actively seeking datasets that represent underrepresented groups and scenarios. By expanding the demographic and contextual diversity of data, AI systems can be trained to recognize and adapt to a broader range of inputs, thereby reducing bias and enhancing generalization across diverse environments.

Another innovative solution is the use of synthetic data. Generative models can simulate diverse scenarios when real-world data is scarce or difficult to obtain. This technique not only supplements existing datasets but also allows for the creation of hypothetical scenarios that can test AI models' robustness and adaptability. For instance, synthetic data can help in modeling rare events or edge cases that are not well-represented in the available data.

Cross-domain collaboration is also a key strategy in promoting data diversity. By partnering with organizations across different industries and regions, AI developers can access a wide array of datasets. This collaboration expands the scope of data inputs and helps in uncovering new insights that might not be apparent within a single domain. Such partnerships can foster innovation and lead to the development of more nuanced AI applications that are sensitive to varying contextual needs.

Bias auditing and the establishment of metrics are critical in maintaining data diversity. Regular evaluations of datasets using specialized tools can identify gaps and biases, allowing for corrective measures to be implemented. By continuously monitoring data inputs, organizations can ensure that their AI models remain fair and unbiased. This ongoing process is essential for maintaining the integrity and trustworthiness of AI systems.

Federated learning presents a promising approach to leveraging diverse data sources while maintaining privacy and security. This method enables decentralized data processing, allowing AI models to learn from data stored locally across multiple devices or locations without the need to centralize the data. This not only preserves privacy but also facilitates the inclusion of diverse data points that might otherwise be inaccessible due to regulatory constraints.

Incorporating these solutions not only addresses the technical challenges of data diversity but also aligns with ethical and governance considerations. Adhering to principles of fairness, accountability, and transparency ensures compliance with data protection regulations and fosters stakeholder trust. By embracing these approaches, AI systems can be developed to serve diverse global needs more effectively and ethically, ultimately leading to more robust and impactful technological advancements.

Regulatory Implications

As the integration of artificial intelligence (AI) and emerging technologies becomes more pervasive, the regulatory landscape faces unprecedented challenges and opportunities. The implications of regulatory frameworks on data diversity in AI are complex, requiring a nuanced understanding of both technological advancements and legislative measures. Policymakers are tasked with balancing innovation with the protection of individual rights and societal norms. This balance is crucial to fostering an environment where AI can thrive while ensuring that its benefits are equitably distributed.

One of the primary concerns in regulating AI is addressing biases that arise from non-diverse data sets. Regulatory bodies must ensure that AI systems are trained on diverse datasets to minimize bias and promote fairness. This involves setting standards for data collection and processing that prioritize inclusivity. Regulations should mandate transparency in how data is sourced and used, ensuring that AI systems do not perpetuate existing inequalities.

The General Data Protection Regulation (GDPR) in Europe serves as a pivotal example of how data privacy laws can influence AI development. GDPR emphasizes the importance of consent and the right to access personal data, which has significant implications for AI systems reliant on large datasets. Compliance with such regulations requires companies to implement robust data management practices, potentially limiting the types of data available for training AI models. However, these constraints also push for innovation in creating synthetic data and other privacy-preserving technologies.

Beyond privacy, regulatory implications extend to the ethical use of AI. There is a growing demand for AI systems to be transparent and accountable. Regulatory frameworks need to establish clear guidelines for ethical AI, encompassing issues such as decision-making processes, explainability, and the ability to audit AI systems. These guidelines are essential for maintaining public trust and ensuring that AI technologies are used responsibly.

Moreover, the international nature of AI development necessitates cooperation across borders. Regulatory bodies must work together to create harmonized standards that facilitate innovation while protecting individuals worldwide. This cooperation can help prevent a fragmented regulatory landscape that could hinder the global potential of AI technologies.

In addition, the rapid pace of AI advancements poses a challenge for regulatory frameworks that are often slow to adapt. Continuous dialogue between technologists and regulators is essential to keep regulations relevant and effective. This dialogue should focus on identifying emerging risks and opportunities, ensuring that regulations evolve in tandem with technological progress.

Finally, regulatory implications are not limited to constraints but also involve enabling technologies. Governments can play a proactive role in promoting data diversity by investing in public datasets and supporting initiatives that encourage diverse data collection. By doing so, they can help create a more equitable AI ecosystem that benefits all sectors of society.

In summary, the regulatory implications of data diversity in AI and emerging technologies are multifaceted. They encompass legal, ethical, and societal dimensions, all of which must be addressed to harness the full potential of AI. By establishing comprehensive and forward-thinking regulatory frameworks, we can ensure that AI technologies are developed and deployed in a manner that is both innovative and socially responsible.

Chapter 7: Data Availability and Quality
Scarcity of Diverse Datasets

In the realm of artificial intelligence and emerging technologies, the availability of diverse datasets is a cornerstone of developing robust and equitable systems. Yet, the scarcity of such datasets poses significant challenges. This scarcity is not merely a logistical hurdle but a fundamental issue that impacts the efficacy and fairness of AI solutions. The lack of diverse datasets can lead to biased models that fail to generalize across different demographics, environments, and cultural contexts. As AI systems are increasingly deployed in various sectors, from healthcare to autonomous vehicles, the need for diverse data becomes ever more critical.

The absence of diverse datasets often stems from several intertwined factors. One primary reason is the bias inherent in data collection processes. Often, data is collected from easily accessible sources, which may not represent the full spectrum of potential users or scenarios. For instance, data gathered from urban areas may overlook rural needs or conditions, leading to models that are ill-equipped to serve a broader audience. Similarly, datasets lacking in demographic diversity might result in AI systems that do not perform well across different age groups, genders, or ethnicities.

Another contributing factor to the scarcity of diverse datasets is the high cost and complexity involved in gathering them. Collecting data that spans various demographics, environments, and contexts requires substantial resources and infrastructure. This can be particularly challenging for smaller organizations or those operating in niche sectors where data is not readily available. Moreover, the legal and ethical constraints surrounding data privacy further complicate the acquisition of diverse datasets. Regulations such as GDPR and CCPA impose strict guidelines on data usage, necessitating that organizations navigate a complex landscape to ensure compliance while striving to enrich their datasets.

The impact of not addressing this scarcity is profound. AI models trained on homogeneous datasets are prone to biases that can perpetuate inequalities and lead to unfair outcomes. For example, facial recognition systems trained predominantly on lighter skin tones have been shown to have lower accuracy rates for individuals with darker skin. Such biases can have real-world consequences, from misidentification in security applications to biased decision-making in financial services.

To mitigate these issues, several strategies can be employed to enhance data diversity. One approach is inclusive data sourcing, which involves actively seeking out data from underrepresented groups and contexts. This requires a concerted effort to broaden the scope of data collection beyond the usual suspects. Another promising avenue is the use of synthetic data generated through advanced techniques like generative adversarial networks (GANs). Synthetic data can simulate scenarios that are difficult to capture in the real world, providing a valuable supplement to existing datasets.

Cross-domain collaboration also plays a vital role in overcoming data scarcity. By partnering with organizations across different industries and regions, it is possible to access a wider array of datasets. Such collaborations can facilitate the sharing of resources and expertise, leading to more comprehensive data solutions. Additionally, the implementation of federated learning allows for the use of decentralized data sources, enabling organizations to leverage diverse datasets without compromising privacy and security.

In conclusion, addressing the scarcity of diverse datasets is imperative for the advancement of AI and emerging technologies. By implementing strategic measures to enhance data diversity, it is possible to develop AI systems that are more equitable, effective, and representative of the diverse world they are designed to serve.

Quality Assessment

Quality assessment in data diversity for AI and emerging technologies plays a crucial role in ensuring that AI models perform optimally across varied environments and demographics. A comprehensive quality assessment involves evaluating the data used in training, validating, and testing AI systems to guarantee its inclusiveness, fairness, and effectiveness. The quality of data directly influences the robustness and bias of AI systems, making it imperative to thoroughly assess the diversity of data.

To begin with, demographic diversity must be scrutinized. This includes ensuring a balanced representation of age, gender, ethnicity, socioeconomic status, and geographic locations. Such diversity is essential to avoid systemic biases that might skew AI outputs. Similarly, contextual diversity, which encompasses variations in environments such as urban versus rural settings, different cultural contexts, and varied use cases, is equally important. This type of diversity ensures that AI systems can adapt to and perform well in diverse real-world scenarios.

Temporal diversity is another critical aspect of data quality assessment. It involves collecting data over different time periods to capture trends and seasonal variations, which can significantly affect the performance of AI models. For instance, data collected during different seasons or across several years can provide insights into long-term trends and changes, thereby enhancing the predictive power of AI systems.

Moreover, domain-specific diversity should not be overlooked. This pertains to the variation in data specific to industries such as healthcare, manufacturing, or education. For example, in the healthcare domain, diverse medical records are necessary to improve diagnostic accuracy across different populations. Similarly, in the field of natural language processing, multilingual and culturally varied data are crucial for developing robust language models.

The challenges in achieving data diversity often stem from biases in data collection, scarcity of diverse datasets, cost and complexity of managing such datasets, and regulatory constraints. These challenges necessitate the implementation of strategies like inclusive data sourcing, the use of synthetic data, cross-domain collaborations, and regular bias auditing. Synthetic data, for example, can simulate diverse scenarios when real-world data is limited, thereby broadening the scope of data diversity.

Incorporating federated learning can also contribute to quality data assessment by enabling the use of decentralized data sources while maintaining privacy and security. This approach not only enhances the diversity of data but also ensures compliance with data protection regulations.

Overall, quality assessment in data diversity is foundational for creating AI systems that are not only technically robust but also ethically sound and socially responsible. By ensuring that AI models are trained and tested on diverse datasets, developers and researchers can mitigate biases, improve generalization, and foster innovation. This, in turn, leads to the development of AI technologies that are capable of serving a wide range of global needs effectively.

Data Sourcing Challenges

The acquisition of data, pivotal for the advancement of AI and emerging technologies, presents an array of challenges that must be navigated to ensure the robustness and inclusivity of AI systems. One prominent concern is the inherent bias in data collection processes.

Systemic biases can lead to the underrepresentation of certain groups or scenarios, often stemming from limited access to diverse data sources. This lack of representation can skew AI models, affecting their fairness and accuracy when deployed in real-world situations.

Additionally, the availability of diverse, high-quality datasets is a significant hurdle, particularly in specialized domains. The scarcity of such datasets can impede the development of AI models capable of generalizing across varied contexts. This is compounded by the cost and complexity associated with gathering and managing these diverse datasets. The resource-intensive nature of this process can be a barrier, especially for smaller organizations or those operating in niche sectors.

Moreover, regulatory and privacy constraints pose significant challenges. Navigating the legal and ethical landscape to access sensitive or protected data requires careful consideration and adherence to data protection regulations. These constraints can limit the scope of data available for AI training, impacting the breadth and depth of data diversity that can be achieved.

Despite these challenges, addressing them is crucial for the benefits they confer. Diverse datasets improve the generalization capabilities of AI models, enabling them to perform effectively across a myriad of real-world scenarios. They also play a critical role in bias mitigation, ensuring that AI systems make fair and equitable decisions. Furthermore, the inclusion of diverse data can drive innovation, leading to novel applications and insights that might otherwise remain unexplored. This diversity also equips AI systems to handle rare or unexpected inputs, enhancing their resilience to edge cases.

To overcome these challenges, several strategies can be employed. Inclusive data sourcing is essential, requiring active efforts to seek data from underrepresented groups and contexts. Where real-world data is limited, synthetic data generation can simulate diverse scenarios, providing a valuable supplement. Cross-domain collaboration also offers a pathway to accessing varied datasets, leveraging partnerships across industries and regions.

Regular bias auditing and the use of specialized metrics are vital in evaluating datasets for gaps and biases. Such evaluations ensure that datasets remain representative and balanced. Federated learning presents another innovative approach, allowing the use of decentralized data sources while maintaining privacy and security. This decentralized method enables the incorporation of diverse data without compromising individual data privacy.

In conclusion, while data sourcing presents formidable challenges, addressing them is imperative for the development of inclusive and effective AI systems. Through strategic efforts to enhance data diversity, AI technologies can achieve their full potential, serving diverse global needs with fairness and accuracy.

Improving Data Quality

Data quality is a cornerstone of effective artificial intelligence and emerging technologies. Ensuring high data quality involves a series of strategic actions aimed at enhancing the usability, accuracy, and reliability of datasets used in training and deploying AI models. One key aspect of improving data quality is the meticulous process of data cleaning. This involves identifying and rectifying errors, inconsistencies, and inaccuracies within datasets. By doing so, organizations can eliminate noise and improve the signal, ensuring that AI models are trained on data that accurately reflects the phenomena they aim to model.

Another crucial step in enhancing data quality is standardization. This involves creating uniform formats and definitions for data across different sources and domains. Standardization facilitates data integration, enabling seamless combination of datasets from diverse origins. This is particularly important in sectors like healthcare and finance, where data is often collected from various systems that may not naturally align. By adopting standardized protocols, organizations can ensure that data is comparable and consistent, thereby enhancing its quality.

Data enrichment is also a vital component of improving data quality. This process involves augmenting existing datasets with additional information to provide a more comprehensive view. For instance, demographic data might be enriched with socio-economic indicators or geographic information, offering deeper insights and enabling more nuanced analysis. Data enrichment can significantly enhance the predictive power of AI models by providing them with a richer set of inputs.

Quality assurance mechanisms are essential to maintain high standards of data quality. This includes implementing robust validation checks at various stages of the data lifecycle, from collection to processing and analysis. Regular audits and reviews of data processes can identify potential weaknesses and areas for improvement. Furthermore, employing automated tools for continuous monitoring can help in promptly detecting and addressing data quality issues, ensuring that datasets remain reliable over time.

Collaboration across different stakeholders is pivotal in enhancing data quality. This involves engaging data scientists, domain experts, and IT professionals in the process of data management. By leveraging the expertise of these diverse groups, organizations can develop more effective strategies for data collection, cleaning, and validation. Collaborative efforts can also foster innovation in data quality techniques, leading to the development of new methodologies and tools.

Finally, fostering a culture of data stewardship within organizations can significantly impact data quality. This involves cultivating a mindset that values the integrity, security, and ethical use of data. Training programs and awareness initiatives can empower employees to recognize the importance of data quality and equip them with the skills needed to maintain it. By prioritizing data stewardship, organizations can ensure that their data assets are managed responsibly and effectively, laying a solid foundation for the deployment of AI and emerging technologies.

Case Studies

In the realm of artificial intelligence and emerging technologies, the implementation of diverse datasets is critical to developing systems that are inclusive, fair, and effective. The case studies presented in this section illustrate how data diversity can be leveraged across various industries to enhance the performance and reliability of AI applications. By examining these real-world examples, we gain insights into the challenges and benefits associated with integrating diverse data sources.

One notable case study involves the healthcare sector, where the diversity of medical datasets plays a pivotal role in improving diagnostic accuracy. In this scenario, data from different demographic groups, regions, and medical histories are utilized to train AI models. This ensures that diagnostic tools are not biased towards any particular group, thereby providing equitable healthcare solutions. For instance, an AI system trained on a wide range of medical images and patient records can more accurately detect diseases across diverse populations, reducing health disparities.

Another significant example can be found in the development of autonomous systems. These systems, such as self-driving cars, rely heavily on environmental data to navigate safely. By incorporating data from various geographical locations and weather conditions, these systems become more adaptable and resilient. This diversity in data ensures that autonomous vehicles can effectively operate in both urban and rural settings, under different climatic conditions, enhancing their safety and reliability.

In the field of Natural Language Processing (NLP), data diversity is instrumental in creating language models that understand and process multiple languages and dialects. By integrating multilingual and culturally varied datasets, NLP systems become more adept at handling linguistic nuances and cultural contexts. This is particularly beneficial for global applications where understanding local languages and dialects is crucial for effective communication and service delivery.

The retail and marketing industries also benefit significantly from diverse consumer data. By analyzing data from a broad spectrum of consumer demographics and behaviors, companies can develop personalized marketing strategies that cater to a global audience. This diversity in consumer data allows businesses to understand and predict purchasing patterns across different regions and cultures, leading to more targeted and effective marketing campaigns.

These case studies underscore the importance of data diversity in AI and emerging technologies. They illustrate how diverse datasets contribute to the development of robust, fair, and inclusive AI systems that cater to a wide range of applications and user needs. However, achieving such diversity is not without its challenges. Issues such as data collection biases, data availability, and regulatory constraints must be addressed to harness the full potential of data diversity.

In conclusion, these examples highlight the transformative impact of data diversity on the effectiveness of AI systems. By continuing to prioritize and integrate diverse data sources, industries can ensure that their AI applications are not only innovative but also equitable and reliable across different contexts and populations.

Chapter 8: Ethical and Governance Considerations
Ethical Principles

In the realm of artificial intelligence and emerging technologies, ethical principles serve as the cornerstone for ensuring that these systems are developed and deployed responsibly. The integration of diverse datasets in AI systems is critical to achieving fairness, accountability, and transparency. These principles guide the creation of algorithms that do not perpetuate bias but instead promote inclusivity across various demographics and contexts.

Fairness is a central ethical consideration, demanding that AI systems treat all individuals and groups equitably. This involves actively identifying and mitigating biases that may arise from skewed data samples. For instance, when training an AI model, it is imperative to include data from a wide range of demographic groups, ensuring that the model performs equally well for all users, regardless of their age, gender, ethnicity, or socioeconomic status. This approach helps prevent discriminatory outcomes that could marginalize certain groups.

Accountability in AI systems involves establishing clear lines of responsibility for the outcomes produced by these technologies. Developers and organizations must be transparent about how data is collected, processed, and used in AI models. This transparency extends to the documentation of data sources and the methodologies employed in model training and validation. By maintaining detailed records, stakeholders can trace decisions back to their data origins, enabling a thorough understanding of the factors influencing AI behavior.

Transparency is closely linked to accountability and is essential for building trust with users and stakeholders. It requires that AI systems be understandable and interpretable by those who use them. This means providing clear explanations of how AI models arrive at their decisions and ensuring that these explanations are accessible to non-expert users. Transparency also involves open communication about the limitations of AI systems, including any potential biases or uncertainties inherent in the models.

The ethical use of diverse data in AI also encompasses privacy and data protection. Adhering to regulations such as the General Data Protection Regulation (GDPR) and the California Consumer Privacy Act (CCPA) is crucial in safeguarding personal information and maintaining public trust. Ethical principles dictate that data should be collected and used with the explicit consent of individuals, and measures should be in place to protect this data from unauthorized access or misuse.

Moreover, stakeholder engagement is a vital component of ethical AI development. By involving a broad spectrum of individuals and groups in the design and implementation of AI systems, developers can ensure that diverse perspectives are considered. This collaborative approach helps identify potential ethical issues early in the development process and fosters a sense of ownership and trust among stakeholders.

In summary, ethical principles in AI and emerging technologies are not merely theoretical ideals but practical guidelines that shape the development and deployment of these systems. By prioritizing fairness, accountability, transparency, privacy, and stakeholder engagement, developers can create AI technologies that are not only innovative but also equitable and trustworthy. These principles ensure that AI systems are designed to serve the diverse needs of global populations, ultimately contributing to a more inclusive and just technological landscape.

Accountability and Transparency

In the realm of artificial intelligence and emerging technologies, the principles of accountability and transparency are vital to ensuring that systems operate ethically and effectively. These principles serve as the bedrock for building trust among users and stakeholders, providing reassurance that AI systems are not only performing their functions as intended but are also doing so in a manner that is fair and just.

Accountability in AI refers to the obligation of organizations and individuals to take responsibility for the outcomes generated by AI systems. This involves establishing clear lines of responsibility and ownership throughout the lifecycle of AI models, from development to deployment. By doing so, organizations can ensure that there are mechanisms in place to address any unintended consequences that may arise. This can include setting up protocols for incident reporting, implementing corrective actions, and maintaining open channels of communication with affected parties.

Transparency, on the other hand, involves the openness and clarity with which AI systems and their decision-making processes are communicated to users. This can be achieved through several strategies, such as providing detailed documentation of AI models, making code and data publicly available where feasible, and using interpretable machine learning techniques that allow users to understand how decisions are made. Transparency is crucial for enabling users to make informed decisions about how they interact with AI systems and for fostering public trust.

Together, accountability and transparency help mitigate risks associated with AI deployment. By ensuring that systems are accountable, organizations can better manage the ethical and legal implications of AI, preventing harm and maintaining compliance with regulations. Transparency further supports this by providing the information necessary to scrutinize AI systems, ensuring they adhere to ethical standards and do not perpetuate biases. This is particularly important in scenarios where AI systems are used in critical areas such as healthcare, criminal justice, and finance, where the stakes are high and the potential for harm is significant.

Moreover, the integration of accountability and transparency into AI systems supports the broader goal of ethical AI. It aligns with the principles of fairness, ensuring that AI systems do not discriminate against individuals or groups. It also promotes the inclusivity of diverse perspectives in the development and deployment of AI, ensuring that a wide range of societal needs and values are considered. This is particularly relevant in the context of data diversity, where diverse datasets are used to train AI models, helping to ensure that these systems are robust and effective across different populations and scenarios.

In summary, accountability and transparency are not merely optional features of AI systems; they are essential components that underpin the ethical deployment of AI technologies. By embedding these principles into the fabric of AI development, organizations can create systems that are not only technically proficient but also socially responsible, thereby fostering a future where AI contributes positively to society.

Compliance with Regulations

Navigating the regulatory landscape is a crucial aspect of implementing data diversity in AI and emerging technologies. This involves understanding and adhering to various legal frameworks and guidelines that govern data use, privacy, and security. As AI systems increasingly influence critical areas such as healthcare, finance, and public policy, ensuring compliance with regulations becomes paramount to building trust and maintaining ethical standards.

One of the primary regulations impacting data diversity initiatives is the General Data Protection Regulation (GDPR) in the European Union. GDPR mandates strict guidelines on data privacy, requiring organizations to obtain explicit consent from individuals before collecting and processing their data. This regulation emphasizes the need for transparency and accountability in data management practices, which is essential when dealing with diverse datasets that may include sensitive personal information. Organizations must implement robust data governance frameworks to ensure that data diversity efforts do not infringe on individual privacy rights.

Similarly, the California Consumer Privacy Act (CCPA) provides a regulatory framework that protects consumer privacy rights in the United States. CCPA grants individuals the right to know what personal data is being collected about them and how it is used. This regulation underscores the importance of maintaining transparency and providing individuals with control over their data. For AI systems utilizing diverse datasets, compliance with CCPA involves implementing mechanisms that allow users to access, rectify, or delete their data as requested.

Beyond privacy regulations, there are industry-specific guidelines that organizations must consider when leveraging data diversity. In the healthcare sector, for instance, the Health Insurance Portability and

Accountability Act (HIPAA) in the United States sets standards for protecting sensitive patient information. Compliance with HIPAA is crucial when using diverse medical datasets to ensure that patient confidentiality is preserved while enabling innovations in AI-driven healthcare solutions.

Moreover, organizations must be mindful of international regulations and cultural considerations when sourcing diverse data from different regions. This involves understanding the legal and ethical implications of cross-border data transfers and ensuring that data collection practices align with local laws and cultural norms. Collaborating with local stakeholders and experts can provide valuable insights into navigating these complexities effectively.

Incorporating compliance into data diversity strategies also involves regular audits and assessments to identify potential risks and ensure adherence to relevant regulations. This proactive approach helps organizations mitigate legal liabilities and build trust with stakeholders, including customers, partners, and regulatory bodies. By demonstrating a commitment to regulatory compliance, organizations can enhance their reputation and foster a culture of ethical responsibility.

In conclusion, compliance with regulations is a fundamental component of successful data diversity initiatives in AI and emerging technologies. By prioritizing regulatory adherence, organizations can protect individual privacy rights, uphold ethical standards, and navigate the complex legal landscape effectively. This commitment to compliance not only mitigates risks but also paves the way for sustainable and responsible innovation in the AI ecosystem.

Stakeholder Engagement

In the dynamic realm of AI and emerging technologies, engaging stakeholders is a pivotal process that steers the development and deployment of systems towards inclusivity and effectiveness. Stakeholders, encompassing a wide range of individuals and groups, including developers, users, policymakers, and marginalized communities, play a crucial role in shaping technologies that are fair and representative. This engagement ensures that diverse perspectives are considered, ultimately fostering systems that are more equitable and reflective of the societies they serve.

The complexity of AI systems necessitates a multifaceted approach to stakeholder engagement. It begins with identifying who the stakeholders are, a task that requires careful consideration of who is impacted by the technology, both directly and indirectly. This identification process is critical because it highlights voices that are often underrepresented in technology development, such as minority groups or those from different socio-economic backgrounds. By including these voices, developers can gain insights into the potential societal impacts of AI systems, allowing for more comprehensive and inclusive design processes.

Once stakeholders are identified, the next step involves active engagement. This can be achieved through workshops, focus groups, and public consultations, where stakeholders are invited to share their experiences, concerns, and expectations regarding AI technologies. Such interactions provide valuable feedback that can guide the development of technology in a direction that aligns with societal values and needs. Furthermore, these engagements can help identify potential biases and ethical dilemmas early in the development process, allowing for proactive measures to address them.

A significant aspect of stakeholder engagement is the establishment of trust. Trust is built through transparency and accountability, where developers and organizations openly communicate the capabilities, limitations, and implications of AI systems. Providing clear and accessible information about how data is collected, used, and protected is essential in maintaining stakeholder confidence. Moreover, demonstrating a commitment to ethical standards and regulatory compliance reassures stakeholders that their interests and rights are safeguarded.

Incorporating stakeholder feedback into the iterative design process of AI systems not only enhances their functionality but also ensures they are culturally and contextually appropriate. This iterative process involves continuously refining and adapting technologies based on stakeholder input, which can lead to more robust and adaptable systems. Such adaptability is crucial in a world where technological advancements and societal needs are constantly evolving.

Furthermore, stakeholder engagement can drive innovation by introducing diverse perspectives and ideas that challenge conventional thinking. This diversity of thought can inspire novel solutions and applications of AI technologies, ultimately broadening their impact and utility. By fostering an environment where all voices are heard and valued, organizations can harness the full potential of human creativity and ingenuity.

In essence, stakeholder engagement is not a one-time event but an ongoing dialogue that evolves alongside technological advancements. It is a critical component in the responsible development of AI and emerging technologies, ensuring that these systems are not only technologically advanced but also socially and ethically aligned with the diverse needs of the global community.

Building Trust

In the realm of artificial intelligence and emerging technologies, the establishment of trust is a pivotal factor that influences the adoption and success of these systems. Trust in AI systems is not merely about ensuring that they function correctly; it encompasses a broader spectrum of ethical, social, and technical dimensions.

A critical aspect of building trust is transparency. Transparency involves making AI systems understandable to users and stakeholders. This includes clear communication about how decisions are made, what data is used, and how algorithms are trained. By demystifying the processes behind AI systems, developers can alleviate fears of hidden biases or malfunctions, thereby fostering trust among users.

Another fundamental component is accountability. AI systems must be designed with mechanisms that allow for tracking and auditing of decisions. This means implementing robust logging and monitoring systems that can provide explanations for AI behavior. When users know that there is a system in place to hold AI accountable, trust is more likely to be established.

Moreover, the ethical use of data is paramount in building trust. AI systems rely heavily on data, and the ethical considerations surrounding data usage are crucial. Ensuring data privacy, obtaining consent for data use, and maintaining data integrity are all essential practices. Users must feel confident that their data is being used responsibly and that their privacy is protected.

Engagement with diverse communities also plays a significant role in trust-building. Involving a wide range of stakeholders in the design and implementation of AI systems ensures that the needs and concerns of different user groups are addressed. This inclusivity helps in creating systems that are fair and unbiased, which is a cornerstone of trust.

Furthermore, cultural sensitivity is essential in the global deployment of AI technologies. AI systems should be adaptable to different cultural contexts and languages. This adaptability not only enhances the usability of the systems but also ensures that they are respectful and considerate of cultural differences, thereby reinforcing trust.

Trust is also built through the demonstration of reliability and consistency. AI systems must perform reliably under various conditions and provide consistent results. This reliability can be achieved through rigorous testing and validation processes that ensure the AI systems meet high standards of performance.

Finally, continuous improvement and adaptation are key to maintaining trust over time. As AI technologies evolve, so too must the systems and policies that govern them. Regular updates and improvements based on user feedback and technological advancements ensure that AI systems remain relevant, effective, and trustworthy.

Building trust in AI and emerging technologies is a multifaceted challenge that requires a comprehensive approach. By prioritizing transparency, accountability, ethical data use, inclusivity, cultural sensitivity, reliability, and continuous improvement, developers and organizations can create AI systems that are trusted by users and beneficial to society as a whole.

Chapter 9: Synthetic Data and Simulation
Generative Models

Generative models have emerged as a cornerstone in the realm of artificial intelligence, offering a paradigm that extends beyond traditional deterministic algorithms. These models are designed to generate new data instances that resemble a given dataset, providing a robust mechanism to simulate complex data distributions. At the heart of generative models is the ability to learn the underlying structure of the input data, which allows them to create realistic and diverse outputs. This capability is particularly beneficial in scenarios where data is scarce or difficult to obtain, making generative models a valuable tool in promoting data diversity in AI.

The architecture of generative models typically involves two main components: a generator and a discriminator, as seen in Generative Adversarial Networks (GANs). The generator creates data instances, while the discriminator evaluates their authenticity. Through a process of adversarial training, these components iteratively improve, resulting in a model that can produce highly realistic data. This adversarial process is akin to a game where the generator tries to fool the discriminator, and the discriminator tries to distinguish between real and generated data. The outcome is a sophisticated model capable of generating data that is nearly indistinguishable from real-world data.

In addition to GANs, other generative models such as Variational Autoencoders (VAEs) and autoregressive models have contributed significantly to the field. VAEs, for instance, provide a probabilistic approach to data generation, capturing the latent variables that define the data distribution. This approach allows for smooth interpolation between data points and the generation of new instances that maintain the intrinsic properties of the training data. Autoregressive models, on the other hand, generate data one step at a time, modeling the probability distribution of each data point conditioned on the previous ones. This sequential approach is particularly effective in tasks such as language modeling and time-series prediction.

The application of generative models extends across various domains, enhancing capabilities in fields such as healthcare, where they can generate synthetic medical data to augment datasets while preserving patient privacy. In the realm of autonomous systems, generative models can simulate diverse environmental conditions, aiding in the training of robust navigation algorithms. Furthermore, in natural language processing, these models are instrumental in generating text that reflects diverse linguistic and cultural contexts, thereby improving the inclusivity and fairness of AI systems.

Despite their potential, generative models also pose challenges, particularly in terms of ethical considerations and the risk of generating misleading or harmful content. It is crucial to implement rigorous evaluation metrics and ethical guidelines to ensure that these models are used responsibly. By doing so, generative models can significantly contribute to data diversity, enabling AI systems to better reflect and serve the multifaceted realities of the world.

Simulating Scenarios

In the realm of artificial intelligence and emerging technologies, the ability to simulate scenarios is a critical component in the development and testing of diverse AI systems. This process involves creating virtual environments and situations that mimic real-world conditions, allowing researchers and developers to observe how AI models respond to various inputs and challenges. These simulations are essential for ensuring that AI systems can operate effectively across a wide range of scenarios, which is crucial for their robustness and reliability.

Simulating scenarios begins with the creation of a comprehensive set of parameters that define the environment in which the AI will operate. These parameters must be meticulously designed to cover a spectrum of variables that the AI might encounter in the real world. This includes variations in demographic data, environmental conditions, and contextual settings. By incorporating such diversity, simulations can reveal potential weaknesses or biases in AI models that might not be apparent in more static testing environments.

One of the primary benefits of simulating scenarios is the ability to test AI systems under controlled yet varied conditions. This approach allows for the identification of edge cases—those rare or extreme situations that can cause AI systems to fail. By exposing AI models to these scenarios during the testing phase, developers can make necessary adjustments to improve the system's resilience and performance.

Moreover, scenario simulation is invaluable for training AI models in environments where real-world data is scarce or difficult to obtain. In such cases, synthetic data generated through simulations can provide a viable alternative. This is particularly relevant in fields like autonomous driving, where collecting real-world data for every possible driving condition is impractical. Simulated scenarios can fill these gaps, providing diverse datasets that help train AI models to handle a wide range of driving conditions safely and effectively.

Another advantage of simulating scenarios is the opportunity it provides for iterative testing and refinement. Developers can run multiple iterations of a scenario, tweaking variables and observing the outcomes, to fine-tune AI models for optimal performance. This iterative process is crucial for developing AI systems that are not only effective but also adaptable to new and unforeseen circumstances.

Furthermore, simulation allows for the exploration of hypothetical situations that have not yet occurred but could potentially arise in the future. This forward-thinking approach enables developers to anticipate and prepare for future challenges, ensuring that AI systems remain relevant and effective as conditions evolve.

In conclusion, the practice of simulating scenarios is an indispensable tool in the development of diverse and robust AI systems. It provides a framework for testing AI models under a wide range of conditions, identifies potential weaknesses, and facilitates the creation of comprehensive training datasets. By leveraging the power of simulation, developers can enhance the reliability and versatility of AI systems, ensuring they meet the demands of an ever-changing world.

Advantages and Limitations

Data diversity presents both significant advantages and notable limitations in the realm of artificial intelligence and emerging technologies. One of the primary advantages of incorporating diverse data is the enhancement of model generalization. When AI models are trained on a wide array of data types, they become adept at handling diverse real-world scenarios, leading to improved performance and reliability. This diversity ensures that AI systems can operate effectively across various environments and populations, thus broadening their applicability and robustness.

Another key benefit is the reduction of algorithmic bias. By integrating diverse datasets, AI systems are less likely to perpetuate existing societal biases, as they are exposed to a wider range of inputs and perspectives. This results in fairer decision-making processes, which is crucial in applications such as hiring, lending, and law enforcement, where bias can have significant ethical and legal implications.

Furthermore, data diversity spurs innovation by providing a rich foundation for discovering novel insights and applications. With access to a broad spectrum of data, researchers and developers can explore new possibilities and create solutions that address previously unmet needs. This can lead to breakthroughs in various fields, from healthcare to autonomous systems, where diverse data can drive the development of more adaptable and efficient technologies.

However, achieving data diversity is not without its challenges. One major limitation is the inherent bias in data collection processes. Systemic issues and limited access to certain data sources can result in the underrepresentation of specific groups or scenarios, which in turn can skew AI outcomes. Addressing these biases requires intentional efforts to source data inclusively and equitably.

Data availability is another significant hurdle. In many specialized domains, diverse, high-quality datasets are scarce, making it difficult to train models that are both comprehensive and accurate. The cost and complexity of gathering and managing such datasets can also be prohibitive, particularly for smaller organizations or those operating in resource-constrained environments.

Additionally, regulatory and privacy constraints pose significant challenges. Legal and ethical considerations often limit access to sensitive or protected data, which can impede efforts to achieve data diversity. Organizations must navigate these constraints carefully to ensure compliance while striving to enhance their datasets.

In summary, while data diversity offers substantial benefits in terms of improving AI model performance, reducing bias, and fostering innovation, it also presents considerable challenges that must be addressed. Balancing these advantages and limitations is crucial for advancing the development of AI and emerging technologies in a way that is both effective and ethical.

Applications in AI

Artificial intelligence (AI) has been a transformative force across various industries, driven by the ability to leverage vast amounts of data. The diversity of this data is crucial for the successful deployment of AI applications, ensuring that models are robust, fair, and applicable across different contexts. By incorporating a wide range of data types and sources, AI systems can better generalize to real-world scenarios, reduce biases, and enhance user experiences.

In healthcare, data diversity is instrumental in improving diagnostic accuracy and treatment effectiveness. Medical records that encompass a broad spectrum of demographics, including different ages, ethnicities, and health conditions, enable the development of AI systems that are more inclusive and precise. This diversity ensures that AI tools do not disproportionately benefit or disadvantage any particular group, thereby promoting health equity.

Autonomous systems, such as self-driving cars, benefit from diverse environmental data. These systems must navigate a variety of terrains, weather conditions, and traffic scenarios. By training AI models on diverse datasets that include urban, rural, and extreme weather conditions, autonomous systems can enhance their adaptability and safety. This diversity is essential for the systems to make accurate decisions in unfamiliar settings, thereby reducing the risk of accidents.

Natural Language Processing (NLP) is another area where data diversity plays a pivotal role. Language models trained on multilingual and culturally varied datasets perform better in understanding and generating human-like text across different languages and cultural contexts. This capability is vital for applications such as translation services, chatbots, and content moderation, where understanding subtle nuances in language can significantly impact user interaction.

In the retail and marketing sectors, diverse consumer data helps create personalized experiences for a global audience. By analyzing data from various consumer demographics and preferences, AI systems can tailor marketing strategies and product recommendations to meet the specific needs and desires of different customer segments. This personalization not only enhances customer satisfaction but also drives business growth by increasing engagement and conversion rates.

The integration of data diversity into AI applications also presents challenges, such as the collection and management of diverse datasets, which can be resource-intensive. Moreover, ensuring data privacy and compliance with regulations like GDPR and CCPA is critical when handling sensitive information. Despite these challenges, the benefits of data diversity in AI applications are substantial, leading to more innovative, fair, and effective technologies.

Overall, the emphasis on data diversity in AI applications highlights the need for inclusive data sourcing strategies, collaboration across sectors, and the utilization of synthetic data to fill gaps where real-world data may be scarce. By addressing these aspects, AI systems can be developed to serve diverse populations effectively, ensuring that technology advancements benefit all of society.

Future Directions

As we look ahead, the landscape of data diversity in AI and emerging technologies presents both challenges and opportunities that demand our attention. One of the primary areas of focus is the integration of more comprehensive datasets that reflect the multifaceted nature of global populations. This involves not only expanding demographic data to include a wider array of ethnicities, ages, and socioeconomic backgrounds but also ensuring that these datasets capture the nuances of different cultural contexts and lived experiences. By doing so, AI systems can be developed to operate more equitably and effectively across a variety of environments.

In addition to broadening demographic data, there is a pressing need to enhance the contextual and temporal diversity of datasets. The inclusion of data from diverse environments—ranging from urban to rural settings—and across different time periods can significantly improve the adaptability and resilience of AI models. This approach helps in capturing seasonal trends and shifts in societal behaviors, which are crucial for applications in areas such as climate modeling and public health.

The future of AI also hinges on overcoming the existing barriers to data diversity, such as the biases inherent in data collection processes. These biases often stem from systemic issues and can lead to the underrepresentation of certain groups or scenarios. Addressing these biases requires a concerted effort to implement bias auditing practices and to develop metrics that can identify and mitigate such disparities. Additionally, the use of synthetic data generated through advanced machine learning techniques offers a promising avenue for simulating diverse scenarios where real-world data may be lacking.

Collaboration across industries and regions will play a pivotal role in fostering data diversity. By establishing partnerships, organizations can share access to varied datasets, enhancing the richness and applicability of AI models. Such collaborations can bridge the gap between different domains, facilitating the cross-pollination of ideas and innovations.

Ethical considerations will continue to be at the forefront of discussions around data diversity. Ensuring compliance with regulations like GDPR and CCPA, while upholding principles of fairness and transparency, is essential for maintaining public trust in AI technologies. Engaging with stakeholders, including communities

111

from which data is sourced, will be crucial in navigating the ethical landscape and addressing societal impacts.

In summary, the future direction of data diversity in AI and emerging technologies will require a multifaceted approach that embraces the complexities of global diversity. By prioritizing the inclusion of comprehensive and representative datasets, addressing biases, and fostering collaborative efforts, we can pave the way for AI systems that are not only innovative but also equitable and socially responsible. This holistic approach will ensure that AI technologies are equipped to meet the diverse needs of a global society, driving progress in a manner that is both inclusive and sustainable.

Chapter 10: Cross-Domain Collaboration
Partnerships Across Industries

The interplay between different industries is crucial in the realm of AI and emerging technologies, where diverse partnerships pave the way for innovative solutions and enhance data diversity. These collaborations are not merely strategic alignments but are fundamental to leveraging the unique strengths each sector offers, thus enriching the data ecosystems essential for developing robust AI models.

Industries such as healthcare, finance, and technology are increasingly recognizing the value of cross-sector partnerships to address complex challenges that no single field can tackle alone. In healthcare, for instance, partnerships with tech companies enable the integration of advanced analytics and AI-driven insights into patient care, leading to improved diagnostic tools and personalized treatment plans. This collaboration is particularly beneficial in aggregating diverse medical datasets, which are critical for training AI systems to be more inclusive and less biased.

The financial sector, too, has seen a surge in partnerships with tech firms to enhance security, streamline operations, and personalize customer experiences. By sharing data and technological expertise, these collaborations facilitate the development of more sophisticated algorithms that can better predict market trends and consumer behaviors, thereby improving decision-making processes.

In the realm of autonomous systems, partnerships across industries such as automotive, technology, and urban planning are essential. These collaborations help in pooling diverse datasets that capture various environmental conditions and user interactions, crucial for training AI systems to navigate real-world scenarios effectively. The diversity in datasets ensures that autonomous systems can operate safely and efficiently across different geographical and cultural contexts.

Moreover, partnerships extend to the educational sector, where collaboration with tech companies can transform traditional learning environments. By integrating AI and machine learning tools, educational institutions can offer personalized learning experiences and predictive analytics to enhance educational outcomes. These partnerships also facilitate access to diverse educational datasets that can be used to train AI models aimed at improving learning methodologies and accessibility.

Retail and marketing sectors are also leveraging cross-industry partnerships to harness the power of AI for personalized customer interactions. By collaborating with data analytics firms, retailers can gain deeper insights into consumer preferences and behaviors, enabling them to tailor their marketing strategies more effectively. This not only enhances customer satisfaction but also drives innovation in product development and service delivery.

The success of these partnerships hinges on a shared commitment to ethical standards and data governance. Industries must ensure that data sharing complies with privacy regulations and ethical guidelines to maintain public trust and safeguard sensitive information. By fostering an environment of transparency and accountability, these collaborations can mitigate the risks associated with data sharing and enhance the overall effectiveness of AI applications.

In conclusion, partnerships across industries are instrumental in advancing the capabilities of AI and emerging technologies. They provide the necessary diversity in data, perspectives, and expertise needed to create AI systems that are not only innovative but also inclusive and fair. As industries continue to collaborate, the potential for transformative solutions and societal benefits grows exponentially, highlighting the indispensable role of these partnerships in shaping the future of technology.

Regional Collaborations

In the rapidly advancing field of artificial intelligence and emerging technologies, the significance of regional collaborations cannot be overstated. These collaborations serve as a catalyst for innovation, fostering an environment where diverse perspectives and expertise converge to address complex challenges. By bridging geographical and cultural divides, regional collaborations enhance the development and deployment of AI technologies that are more inclusive and representative of global diversity.

Regional collaborations in AI and emerging technologies involve partnerships between academic institutions, industry leaders, and government entities within specific geographic areas. These collaborations are designed to leverage local strengths, such as unique datasets, specialized research capabilities, and indigenous knowledge, to create AI solutions that are tailored to the needs of the region. Moreover, they provide a platform for sharing resources, knowledge, and best practices, which accelerates the pace of technological advancement and innovation.

One of the primary benefits of regional collaborations is the pooling of resources and expertise. By working together, organizations can share the financial burden of research and development, access a wider range of technical skills, and benefit from the diverse perspectives that come from different cultural and socio-economic backgrounds. This collaborative approach not only enhances the quality and scope of AI research but also ensures that the resulting technologies are more robust and adaptable to various contexts.

Furthermore, regional collaborations offer a strategic advantage in addressing the ethical and regulatory challenges associated with AI and emerging technologies. Different regions have varying regulations and cultural norms, which can impact the development and implementation of AI systems. By collaborating regionally, stakeholders can develop frameworks and guidelines that are sensitive to local contexts, ensuring compliance with local laws and ethical standards. This localized approach to governance helps build trust among users and stakeholders, facilitating the acceptance and integration of AI technologies into society.

Another critical aspect of regional collaborations is their role in capacity building and talent development. By fostering partnerships between educational institutions and industry, regions can develop targeted training programs that equip the local workforce with the necessary skills to thrive in the AI-driven economy. These programs not only address the immediate demand for AI expertise but also contribute to long-term economic growth and stability by creating a pipeline of skilled professionals who can drive innovation and competitiveness in the region.

Moreover, regional collaborations can act as a testing ground for new technologies and applications. By piloting AI solutions in specific regions, organizations can gather valuable data and insights on user interactions, technical performance, and societal impact. This real-world feedback is crucial for refining AI systems and ensuring they meet the diverse needs of different populations. Successful regional pilots can then be scaled to other areas, demonstrating the global applicability and potential of the technologies developed.

In sum, regional collaborations in AI and emerging technologies are essential for harnessing the full potential of data diversity. They enable the development of AI systems that are not only technically advanced but also culturally and contextually relevant. By fostering an environment of cooperation and shared learning, regional

117

collaborations pave the way for a more inclusive and equitable technological future.

Sharing Diverse Datasets

In the realm of artificial intelligence and emerging technologies, the sharing of diverse datasets has emerged as a pivotal factor in advancing the field. The essence of data diversity lies in its ability to encompass a wide range of demographic, contextual, temporal, and domain-specific variations. This diversity is not merely about quantity but about capturing the rich tapestry of human experience and environmental contexts that AI systems must navigate.

The impetus for sharing diverse datasets stems from a fundamental need to ensure that AI models are inclusive, fair, and effective. By incorporating a broad spectrum of data, AI systems can minimize biases, improve robustness, and enhance their generalization capabilities across different populations and scenarios. This inclusivity is crucial in avoiding the pitfalls of algorithmic bias, which can lead to skewed decision-making processes that disproportionately affect certain groups.

The challenges in sharing diverse datasets are multifaceted. One significant hurdle is the inherent bias in data collection processes, which often results in the underrepresentation of certain groups or scenarios. This underrepresentation can be attributed to systemic issues or limited access to comprehensive data sources. Moreover, the

118

scarcity of diverse, high-quality datasets in specialized domains further complicates the matter, as does the cost and complexity associated with gathering and managing such data. Additionally, regulatory and privacy constraints pose significant barriers, requiring careful navigation of legal and ethical considerations when accessing sensitive or protected data.

Despite these challenges, the benefits of sharing diverse datasets are substantial. Improved generalization across diverse real-world scenarios is a key advantage, as it ensures that AI models are better equipped to handle unexpected inputs and edge cases. This capability is particularly vital in applications such as healthcare, where diverse medical records can lead to more accurate diagnoses across different populations. In autonomous systems, diverse environmental data enhances safety and adaptability, while in natural language processing, multilingual and culturally varied data improve the performance of language models.

To promote the sharing of diverse datasets, several strategies can be employed. Inclusive data sourcing is essential, actively seeking out data from underrepresented groups and contexts to fill existing gaps. When real-world data is limited, synthetic data generated by advanced models can simulate diverse scenarios, providing a viable alternative. Cross-domain collaboration is another effective approach, facilitating partnerships with organizations across different industries and regions to access a wider array of datasets.

Moreover, bias auditing and the use of specialized metrics can help identify and address gaps and biases in datasets. Federated learning offers a promising solution by leveraging decentralized data sources while maintaining privacy and security, thus enabling the sharing of diverse datasets without compromising sensitive information.

The ethical and governance considerations in sharing diverse datasets cannot be overlooked. Adherence to ethical principles such as fairness, accountability, and transparency is paramount. Compliance with data protection regulations, like GDPR and CCPA, ensures that data sharing practices align with legal standards. Engaging stakeholders to address societal impacts and build trust is also crucial in fostering a collaborative environment for data sharing.

Ultimately, the sharing of diverse datasets is foundational in creating robust, ethical, and impactful AI systems capable of serving the diverse needs of a global population effectively.

Challenges and Solutions

In the quest to harness the full potential of artificial intelligence and emerging technologies, data diversity presents a multifaceted challenge that requires innovative solutions. The primary challenge lies in the inherent biases often found in data collection processes. These biases arise from systemic issues or limited access to diverse data sources, leading to the underrepresentation of certain groups or scenarios. This lack of representation can skew AI models, resulting in systems that do not perform equitably across different demographics or contexts. Addressing these biases necessitates a concerted effort to source data inclusively, ensuring that all segments of society are represented in AI training datasets.

Another significant hurdle is the availability of diverse, high-quality datasets, especially in specialized domains. The scarcity of such datasets can limit the ability of AI systems to generalize effectively across real-world scenarios. This limitation underscores the need for cross-domain collaboration, where organizations across industries and regions partner to share and access varied datasets. Such collaborations not only enhance data diversity but also foster innovation by opening up novel applications and insights that are inspired by broader datasets.

The cost and complexity of gathering and managing diverse datasets also pose significant challenges. Collecting data from a wide array of sources can be resource-intensive, requiring substantial investments in time, money, and technology. To mitigate these challenges, the use of synthetic data has emerged as a viable solution. By employing generative models, it is possible to simulate diverse scenarios when real-world data is limited. Synthetic data provides a cost-effective means to enhance data diversity without the constraints of traditional data collection methods.

Moreover, regulatory and privacy constraints often complicate the access to sensitive or protected data, posing ethical and legal challenges. Navigating these constraints requires a careful balance

121

between data utility and privacy protection. Federated learning offers a promising solution by leveraging decentralized data sources while maintaining privacy and security. This approach allows for the training of AI models on diverse datasets without the need to centralize sensitive data, thus adhering to privacy regulations while promoting data diversity.

To ensure that AI systems are robust and fair, it is crucial to implement regular bias auditing and use specialized metrics to evaluate datasets for gaps and biases. This ongoing evaluation helps to identify and rectify imbalances, ensuring that AI systems are fair and effective across diverse populations. Additionally, fostering stakeholder engagement is essential to address societal impacts and build trust in AI technologies. By involving a broad range of stakeholders, it is possible to ensure that AI systems are developed and deployed in a manner that is aligned with ethical principles such as fairness, accountability, and transparency.

Ultimately, the challenges of achieving data diversity in AI and emerging technologies are complex but not insurmountable. Through inclusive data sourcing, synthetic data generation, cross-domain collaboration, and privacy-preserving techniques like federated learning, it is possible to overcome these challenges and build AI systems that are capable of serving diverse global needs effectively.

Case Studies

In the exploration of data diversity within AI and emerging technologies, case studies serve as pivotal examples to illustrate the impact and application of diverse data sets. These case studies reveal how diversity in data can significantly enhance the functionality, fairness, and adaptability of AI systems across various sectors.

Consider the healthcare industry, where the incorporation of diverse medical records from multiple demographics has been shown to improve diagnostic accuracy and treatment outcomes. By including data from a range of ethnicities, ages, and genders, AI models in healthcare can deliver more precise and personalized care. This diversity ensures that the algorithms are not biased towards a particular group, thus fostering equitable healthcare solutions.

In the realm of autonomous systems, such as self-driving cars, data diversity is crucial for safety and reliability. These systems must operate effectively in a wide array of environments, from bustling urban centers to serene rural landscapes. By training AI systems with a diverse array of environmental data, developers can ensure that autonomous vehicles respond appropriately to varying weather conditions, traffic patterns, and unexpected obstacles. This comprehensive approach to data collection helps mitigate risks and enhances the adaptability of autonomous systems in real-world scenarios.

Natural Language Processing (NLP) is another area where data diversity plays a transformative role. Language models benefit immensely from exposure to multilingual and culturally diverse datasets. By incorporating a variety of languages and dialects, NLP systems can improve their understanding and generation of human language, thereby breaking down communication barriers. This diversity enables AI to support global users more effectively, providing more accurate translations and culturally relevant content.

In the fields of retail and marketing, diverse consumer data is leveraged to create personalized and engaging customer experiences. By analyzing data from various consumer segments, businesses can tailor their marketing strategies to meet the unique preferences and needs of different audiences. This approach not only boosts customer satisfaction but also drives sales and fosters brand loyalty across diverse markets.

The case studies underscore the multifaceted benefits of data diversity in AI. They highlight how diverse datasets lead to improved generalization, bias mitigation, and innovative solutions across industries. Furthermore, these examples emphasize the importance of actively seeking and integrating diverse data sources to build robust and fair AI systems. As the technological landscape continues to evolve, the lessons gleaned from these case studies can guide future efforts to harness the full potential of data diversity in AI and emerging technologies.

Chapter 11: Bias Auditing and Metrics
Evaluating Datasets

In the realm of artificial intelligence and emerging technologies, the evaluation of datasets is a critical step that ensures the effectiveness and fairness of AI models. Evaluating datasets involves analyzing the composition and quality of the data used for training, validation, and testing. This process helps identify potential biases and gaps, ensuring that the AI systems developed are robust and applicable across diverse scenarios.

The first aspect of evaluating datasets is understanding the diversity within the data. Diversity encompasses demographic, contextual, temporal, and domain-specific variations. Demographic diversity includes factors such as age, gender, ethnicity, and geographic location, which are essential in creating models that are inclusive and representative of the population. Contextual diversity, on the other hand, involves variations in environments, cultures, and use cases, ensuring that AI systems can adapt to different situational contexts.

Temporal diversity is another crucial factor, as it involves data collected over different time periods. This helps capture trends and seasonal variations, allowing models to remain relevant over time. Domain-specific diversity refers to variations in industry-specific data, such as healthcare records or financial transactions, which are vital for developing specialized AI applications.

A significant challenge in evaluating datasets is addressing the biases that may exist in the data collection process. Biases can arise from underrepresentation of certain groups or scenarios, often due to systemic issues or limited access to data sources. Evaluating datasets involves identifying these biases and implementing strategies to mitigate them, thereby improving the fairness and reliability of AI models.

Data availability is another challenge, as diverse, high-quality datasets can be scarce, particularly in specialized domains. The cost and complexity of gathering and managing such datasets further complicate the evaluation process. Moreover, regulatory and privacy constraints must be considered, as accessing sensitive or protected data involves navigating legal and ethical considerations.

Strategies for effective dataset evaluation include inclusive data sourcing, where efforts are made to obtain data from underrepresented groups and contexts. The use of synthetic data, generated through advanced models, can simulate diverse scenarios when real-world data is limited. Cross-domain collaboration is also beneficial, as partnerships across industries and regions can provide access to varied datasets.

Bias auditing tools and metrics are essential in the evaluation process, allowing for regular assessments of datasets to identify and address gaps and biases. Additionally, federated learning offers a way to leverage decentralized data sources while maintaining privacy and security, further supporting the evaluation process.

In summary, evaluating datasets is a foundational practice in the development of AI systems. It ensures that models are not only technically proficient but also ethically aligned and socially responsible. By focusing on diversity and actively addressing biases, the evaluation of datasets contributes to the creation of AI technologies that are inclusive and effective across a wide range of applications.

Tools and Frameworks

In the realm of artificial intelligence and emerging technologies, the role of tools and frameworks in fostering data diversity is indispensable. As AI systems increasingly permeate various sectors, ensuring these systems are trained on diverse datasets becomes crucial to minimizing bias and enhancing performance across different contexts. Tools and frameworks serve as the backbone for achieving this diversity, providing the necessary infrastructure to collect, process, and analyze a wide array of data types.

A critical aspect of these tools is their ability to handle demographic, contextual, temporal, and domain-specific diversity. Demographic diversity refers to the inclusion of data from various age groups, genders, ethnicities, socioeconomic statuses, and geographic locations. Contextual diversity involves capturing variations in environments, such as urban versus rural settings, and cultural differences. Temporal diversity ensures that data collected over different time periods is considered, capturing trends and seasonal variations. Domain-specific diversity focuses on gathering data pertinent to specific industries, such as healthcare or manufacturing, which may require specialized tools to manage unique data types effectively.

One of the primary challenges in achieving data diversity is the bias inherent in data collection processes. Tools and frameworks are essential in identifying and mitigating these biases. They provide functionalities for auditing datasets, ensuring that underrepresented groups or scenarios are adequately captured. Bias auditing tools, for instance, can evaluate datasets for gaps and biases, offering metrics that highlight areas needing improvement. These tools enable developers to refine their datasets, promoting fairness and inclusivity in AI models.

Moreover, the availability of diverse, high-quality datasets remains a significant hurdle. Here, synthetic data generation frameworks play a pivotal role. By using generative models, these frameworks can simulate diverse scenarios where real-world data is scarce. This approach not only expands the dataset but also introduces variations that may not be present in existing data, thus enhancing model generalization.

Cross-domain collaboration frameworks facilitate partnerships across industries and regions, enabling access to a broader spectrum of data. Such collaborations are crucial for obtaining data that reflects a wide range of real-world conditions, thereby improving AI systems' adaptability and resilience.

Federated learning frameworks offer another innovative approach by allowing decentralized data sources to be utilized while maintaining privacy and security. These frameworks enable models to learn from data distributed across multiple locations without compromising sensitive information, thus supporting data diversity without violating privacy norms.

In addition to these technical solutions, the ethical and governance aspects of data diversity cannot be overlooked. Tools and frameworks that incorporate ethical principles, such as fairness, accountability, and transparency, are vital in building trust with stakeholders. They ensure compliance with data protection regulations and foster engagement with various societal groups, addressing potential impacts and promoting responsible AI development.

Ultimately, the integration of advanced tools and frameworks is essential for advancing data diversity in AI. They provide the means to manage complex datasets, mitigate biases, and ensure that AI systems are robust, fair, and reflective of the diverse world they are designed to serve.

Addressing Gaps

In the rapidly evolving landscape of artificial intelligence and emerging technologies, addressing gaps in data diversity is paramount. The absence of diverse data can lead to biased AI models, which in turn can perpetuate inequalities and reduce the effectiveness of AI systems across various demographics and use cases. To tackle these challenges, a multifaceted approach is necessary, involving both technical and ethical considerations.

Firstly, it is essential to recognize the types of gaps that commonly occur in data diversity. These include demographic gaps, where certain age groups, genders, or ethnicities are underrepresented; contextual gaps, where specific environments or cultural settings are not adequately captured; and temporal gaps, which arise when data is not collected over sufficient time periods to account for trends and seasonal variations. Each of these gaps can significantly impact the generalization ability of AI models, leading to skewed outcomes that fail to serve the broader population.

To address these gaps, organizations must adopt inclusive data sourcing strategies. This involves actively seeking out data from underrepresented groups and contexts, ensuring that the datasets used to train AI models are reflective of the diversity found in real-world scenarios. In cases where real-world data is scarce or difficult to obtain, synthetic data generation can be a valuable tool. By using generative models, it is possible to simulate a wide range of scenarios and conditions, thereby enriching the training datasets with the necessary diversity.

Cross-domain collaboration is another effective strategy for addressing data diversity gaps. By partnering with organizations across different industries and regions, it becomes possible to access a wider array of datasets. This collaborative approach not only enhances the richness of the data but also fosters innovation by exposing AI systems to novel applications and insights. Furthermore, federated learning presents an opportunity to leverage decentralized data sources while maintaining privacy and security, thus overcoming some of the regulatory and ethical challenges associated with data sharing.

Regular bias auditing and the use of specialized metrics are crucial for identifying and addressing gaps in datasets. By continuously evaluating data for potential biases, organizations can implement corrective measures to ensure fairness and inclusivity in AI models. This process is supported by the development of tools and frameworks specifically designed to detect and mitigate biases, thereby enhancing the overall robustness of AI systems.

The implications of addressing data diversity gaps extend beyond technical performance. Ethically, it is vital to adhere to principles of fairness, accountability, and transparency. Compliance with data protection regulations, such as GDPR and CCPA, is necessary to safeguard privacy and build trust among stakeholders. Moreover, engaging with diverse communities and stakeholders is essential for understanding the societal impacts of AI and ensuring that the benefits of technological advancements are equitably distributed.

Ultimately, addressing gaps in data diversity is not merely a technical challenge but a fundamental aspect of developing AI systems that are ethical, inclusive, and capable of serving the diverse needs of a global population. By prioritizing diversity in data collection and model training, the AI community can pave the way for more equitable and effective technological solutions.

Regular Audits

In the rapidly evolving landscape of artificial intelligence and emerging technologies, the importance of maintaining data diversity cannot be overstated. Regular audits play a crucial role in ensuring that data diversity is upheld, serving as a mechanism to identify and mitigate biases, enhance fairness, and improve the robustness of AI systems. These audits are systematic evaluations of datasets and the processes by which they are collected, curated, and utilized. By conducting regular audits, organizations can ensure that their AI systems remain inclusive and effective across various demographics, contexts, and scenarios.

Regular audits are essential for identifying gaps in data diversity. AI systems are often trained on datasets that may inadvertently reflect societal biases, leading to skewed outcomes that can perpetuate inequality. Through audits, these biases can be detected early, allowing for corrective measures to be implemented. This not only enhances the fairness of AI systems but also their generalizability, as models trained on diverse datasets are better equipped to handle a wide array of real-world situations.

Moreover, regular audits contribute to the ongoing improvement of data collection practices. They encourage the adoption of inclusive data sourcing strategies, which involve actively seeking out data from underrepresented groups and environments. This proactive approach helps to fill the gaps identified during audits, ensuring that datasets are more representative of the diverse populations that AI systems are intended to serve. Additionally, audits can evaluate the effectiveness of synthetic data generation, which is used to simulate diverse scenarios when real-world data is scarce.

The process of conducting regular audits involves several key steps. Firstly, organizations must define clear metrics and criteria for evaluating data diversity. These metrics should consider various dimensions of diversity, including demographic, contextual, temporal, and domain-specific factors. Once these criteria are established, datasets can be systematically reviewed to assess their compliance with these standards. This review process often involves the use of specialized tools and frameworks designed to detect and quantify biases within datasets.

Another critical aspect of regular audits is the evaluation of data governance practices. Ensuring compliance with legal and ethical standards, such as data protection regulations and ethical principles of fairness and accountability, is paramount. Audits provide an opportunity to review these practices, ensuring that data is collected, stored, and used in a manner that respects individuals' rights and fosters trust among stakeholders.

Finally, regular audits serve as a foundation for fostering innovation in AI and emerging technologies. By ensuring that datasets are diverse and free from bias, organizations can unlock new insights and applications that reflect the needs and values of a broader audience. This not only enhances the societal impact of AI systems but also supports their commercial viability by opening up new markets and opportunities.

In summary, regular audits are a vital component of maintaining data diversity in AI and emerging technologies. They provide a structured approach to identifying and addressing biases, improving data collection practices, and ensuring compliance with ethical and legal standards. Through these audits, organizations can create AI systems that are more inclusive, fair, and effective, ultimately leading to more equitable and impactful technological advancements.

Best Practices

In the rapidly evolving landscape of artificial intelligence and emerging technologies, ensuring data diversity is a pivotal element in the development of robust and fair AI systems. The concept of data diversity encompasses the inclusion of various demographic, contextual, temporal, and domain-specific data, each contributing to a comprehensive dataset that reflects the multifaceted nature of real-world scenarios. By embracing data diversity, AI systems can achieve higher levels of inclusivity, fairness, and effectiveness across diverse populations.

A primary benefit of data diversity is improved generalization. AI models trained on diverse datasets are better equipped to perform effectively across a wide range of real-world situations. This generalization capability is crucial in minimizing bias, a common issue that arises when models are trained on homogenous data. By incorporating a variety of data types, including those that represent underrepresented groups or uncommon scenarios, AI systems can mitigate algorithmic bias, ensuring fairness in decision-making processes.

Furthermore, data diversity fosters innovation by broadening the spectrum of datasets available for analysis. With access to a wider array of data, researchers and developers can uncover novel insights and applications, driving advancements in technology and methodology. This enhanced innovation is accompanied by an increased resilience to edge cases, as systems trained on diverse data are better prepared to handle rare or unexpected inputs.

To effectively promote data diversity, several strategies can be employed. Inclusive data sourcing is essential, involving the active pursuit of data from underrepresented groups and contexts. This approach ensures that the datasets used in AI development are reflective of the diverse world we live in. Additionally, synthetic data generation can be utilized to simulate diverse scenarios, particularly when real-world data is scarce or difficult to obtain. This method leverages generative models to create realistic data that fills gaps in existing datasets.

Cross-domain collaboration is another vital strategy, encouraging partnerships between organizations across different industries and regions. Such collaborations provide access to varied datasets, enriching the diversity of data available for AI training. Furthermore, bias auditing and the implementation of specialized metrics are critical in regularly evaluating datasets for potential gaps and biases. These tools and frameworks help maintain the integrity of datasets, ensuring that they remain representative and fair.

Federated learning offers a decentralized approach to data diversity, allowing for the integration of data from multiple sources while maintaining privacy and security. This method is particularly beneficial in scenarios where data cannot be centralized due to regulatory or privacy constraints.

Incorporating data diversity into AI systems also necessitates adherence to ethical and governance considerations. Ensuring compliance with data protection regulations, such as GDPR and CCPA, is paramount. Additionally, fostering stakeholder engagement is crucial in addressing societal impacts and building trust in AI systems. By prioritizing fairness, accountability, and transparency, developers can create AI systems that are not only technologically advanced but also ethically sound.

Overall, data diversity is a foundational aspect of developing AI systems that are robust, ethical, and capable of serving diverse global needs. By adopting best practices in data diversity, the AI community can contribute to the creation of technologies that are both innovative and equitable, ultimately leading to a more inclusive technological future.

Chapter 12: Federated Learning
Decentralized Data Sources

In the landscape of artificial intelligence and emerging technologies, the concept of decentralized data sources is gaining traction as a pivotal element in promoting data diversity. The reliance on centralized data repositories often presents challenges such as bottlenecks in data access, issues related to privacy, and potential biases due to the limited scope of data collection. Decentralized data sources offer a compelling alternative by distributing data collection and storage across a network, thereby enhancing the inclusivity and representativeness of datasets.

Decentralization facilitates the inclusion of a wide array of data types from diverse geographic and demographic backgrounds. This is particularly crucial in AI development, where the effectiveness and fairness of models are significantly influenced by the diversity of training data. By tapping into decentralized sources, developers can access data that reflects a broader spectrum of societal variables, such as different cultural contexts, languages, and socioeconomic conditions. This diversity is instrumental in crafting AI systems that are more generalizable and less prone to bias.

One of the primary advantages of decentralized data sources is their ability to enhance data privacy and security. In a decentralized network, data is often stored locally and processed using techniques such as federated learning. This approach allows for model training on local devices without the need to transfer sensitive data to a central server.

As a result, individuals retain greater control over their personal data, aligning with stringent data protection regulations such as GDPR and CCPA.

Moreover, decentralized data sources can lead to improved data resilience. In a centralized system, a single point of failure can compromise data integrity and availability. Conversely, decentralization disperses data across multiple nodes, reducing the risk of data loss and ensuring continuous access even if some nodes are compromised. This resilience is particularly beneficial in sectors like healthcare and finance, where data availability is critical.

Decentralized networks also foster innovation by enabling the integration of diverse data streams. For example, in smart cities, decentralized data sources can aggregate information from various sensors and devices, facilitating more efficient urban planning and management. Similarly, in personalized medicine, decentralized platforms can combine patient data from multiple sources to improve treatment outcomes.

However, the implementation of decentralized data sources is not without challenges. Technical complexities, such as ensuring interoperability between different systems and maintaining data quality, can pose significant hurdles. Additionally, there are concerns about the scalability of decentralized networks and the computational resources required to manage them.

Despite these challenges, the potential of decentralized data sources to revolutionize data diversity in AI and emerging technologies is undeniable. By fostering a more inclusive and secure data ecosystem, decentralization not only enhances the robustness of AI models but also democratizes access to data, empowering individuals and communities to contribute to and benefit from technological advancements. As the field continues to evolve, embracing decentralized data sources will be key to unlocking new possibilities and ensuring that AI systems are equitable and reflective of the diverse world they serve.

Privacy and Security

The integration of data diversity in AI and emerging technologies brings to the forefront critical considerations surrounding privacy and security. As we harness diverse datasets to train and deploy AI systems, it's imperative to address the inherent privacy risks associated with the collection, storage, and processing of such data. The diversity of data, while beneficial for enhancing AI model accuracy and inclusivity, introduces complexities in ensuring that personal information remains protected.

Privacy concerns in AI are primarily centered around the potential misuse of sensitive data. Diverse datasets often include personal attributes such as demographic information, health records, and social behavior patterns. The aggregation of such data poses risks of re-identification, where anonymized data can be traced back to

141

individuals, thereby compromising privacy. This is particularly concerning in datasets that combine multiple sources of information, each contributing unique identifiers. Therefore, robust anonymization techniques and differential privacy measures are essential to mitigate these risks, ensuring that the data utilized by AI systems cannot be exploited to reveal personal identities.

Security is another critical aspect that must be addressed in the context of data diversity. The more diverse the dataset, the broader the attack surface for potential breaches. AI systems trained on heterogeneous data are susceptible to adversarial attacks, where malicious actors manipulate input data to deceive the AI model. This vulnerability necessitates the implementation of advanced security protocols, such as encryption and secure multi-party computation, to safeguard data integrity and confidentiality throughout the AI lifecycle.

Moreover, regulatory frameworks play a pivotal role in governing privacy and security in AI. Laws such as the General Data Protection Regulation (GDPR) and the California Consumer Privacy Act (CCPA) impose stringent requirements on data handling processes, emphasizing the need for transparency and user consent. Compliance with these regulations is not merely a legal obligation but a strategic imperative for organizations aiming to build trust with stakeholders and users. Ensuring that AI systems align with these regulations involves conducting regular privacy impact assessments and adopting privacy-by-design principles in system development.

The ethical implications of privacy and security in AI extend beyond compliance. Organizations must foster a culture of accountability, where data protection is prioritized at every level of operation. This involves educating stakeholders about the risks associated with data diversity and the measures in place to address them. Additionally, fostering collaboration with external entities, such as privacy advocacy groups and industry consortia, can provide valuable insights and resources for enhancing data protection strategies.

In addressing privacy and security concerns, the role of technology cannot be understated. Innovations in cryptography and secure data sharing mechanisms are continually evolving, offering new avenues for protecting diverse datasets. Techniques like federated learning, which allows AI models to be trained across decentralized devices without exchanging raw data, exemplify how technological advancements can reconcile data diversity with privacy imperatives.

Ultimately, the balance between leveraging data diversity and ensuring privacy and security is a dynamic challenge that requires ongoing vigilance and adaptation. By prioritizing these aspects, we can develop AI systems that are not only powerful and inclusive but also respectful of individual rights and societal norms.

Benefits for Diversity

In the realm of artificial intelligence and emerging technologies, the concept of data diversity plays a pivotal role in shaping the capabilities and fairness of AI systems. Data diversity encompasses the variety of data used to train, validate, and test AI models, including differences in demographics, languages, cultures, environments, and scenarios. This diversity is crucial for ensuring that AI systems are inclusive, fair, and effective across diverse populations.

One significant benefit of data diversity is improved generalization. AI models trained on diverse datasets demonstrate better performance across a wide array of real-world scenarios. This enhanced generalization is crucial for applications that require adaptability to various contexts, such as autonomous systems and healthcare diagnostics. For instance, in healthcare, diverse medical records allow AI to provide accurate diagnostic results for patients from different backgrounds, thereby improving healthcare outcomes on a global scale.

Moreover, data diversity is instrumental in mitigating bias within AI systems. Bias in AI can arise from underrepresentation of certain groups or scenarios, leading to unfair and potentially harmful outcomes. By incorporating diverse datasets, AI systems can reduce algorithmic bias, thereby ensuring fairness in decision-making processes. This is particularly important in applications like natural language processing (NLP), where multilingual and culturally varied data can significantly enhance the accuracy and fairness of language models.

Another advantage is the potential for enhanced innovation. Diverse datasets provide a broader spectrum of information, inspiring novel applications and insights. This diversity fosters creativity and innovation, as it enables the exploration of new possibilities and the development of solutions that are more attuned to the needs of diverse populations. In industries such as retail and marketing, diverse consumer data allows for the creation of personalized experiences that cater to a global audience, enhancing customer satisfaction and engagement.

Furthermore, data diversity contributes to the resilience of AI systems when encountering edge cases. Systems trained on a wide range of data are better equipped to handle rare or unexpected inputs, improving their robustness and reliability. This resilience is vital in safety-critical applications, such as autonomous vehicles, where the ability to respond appropriately to unforeseen scenarios can prevent accidents and save lives.

To promote data diversity, several strategies can be employed. Inclusive data sourcing involves actively seeking data from underrepresented groups and contexts, ensuring that diverse perspectives are represented in AI training datasets. Additionally, synthetic data generation can simulate diverse scenarios when real-world data is scarce, providing a valuable tool for enhancing data diversity. Cross-domain collaboration between organizations across different industries and regions can also facilitate access to varied datasets, enriching the diversity of data available for AI development.

145

In conclusion, data diversity is foundational for creating robust, ethical, and impactful AI systems that effectively serve diverse global needs. By embracing data diversity, AI developers can ensure that their systems are not only technologically advanced but also equitable and responsive to the complexities of the real world.

Implementation Challenges

The advent of artificial intelligence and emerging technologies has brought to the forefront the critical importance of data diversity. However, the implementation of data diversity in AI systems is fraught with a multitude of challenges that must be addressed to harness its full potential. A primary challenge is the inherent bias present in data collection processes. Often, data is gathered from sources that are not representative of the entire population. This underrepresentation stems from systemic issues or a lack of access to diverse data sources, which can result in AI systems that do not perform equitably across different demographic groups.

In addition to bias, the availability of diverse, high-quality datasets poses a significant hurdle. In many specialized domains, there is a scarcity of comprehensive datasets that encompass the necessary breadth of diversity. This scarcity not only limits the effectiveness of AI models but also restricts their applicability to broader, real-world scenarios. The task of gathering and managing such diverse datasets is complex and resource-intensive, often requiring substantial investments of time and money. This complexity is compounded by regulatory and privacy constraints that govern the access and use of sensitive data, necessitating careful navigation of legal and ethical frameworks.

Furthermore, the cost associated with implementing data diversity is not merely financial. There is also a technological cost, as the integration of diverse datasets demands sophisticated tools and methodologies to ensure that the data is used effectively and ethically. The challenges extend to the technical domain, where the development of algorithms capable of handling diverse inputs without bias is still an evolving field.

Addressing these challenges requires a multifaceted approach. One strategy is inclusive data sourcing, which emphasizes actively seeking out data from underrepresented groups and contexts. This proactive approach can help mitigate the biases inherent in traditional data collection methods. Additionally, the use of synthetic data—generated through advanced generative models—offers a promising avenue for simulating diverse scenarios when real-world data is limited. Such synthetic data can complement existing datasets, enhancing their diversity and robustness.

Cross-domain collaboration is another effective strategy. By partnering with organizations across different industries and regions, it is possible to access a wider array of datasets, each contributing unique perspectives and insights. This collaborative approach not only enriches the data pool but also fosters innovation and cross-pollination of ideas between sectors.

Moreover, regular auditing of datasets for gaps and biases is crucial. Utilizing specialized tools and frameworks to evaluate data diversity can help identify and address deficiencies, ensuring that AI systems remain fair and inclusive. Federated learning, which leverages decentralized data sources while maintaining privacy and security, is another technique that holds promise for overcoming data diversity challenges.

In summary, while the implementation of data diversity in AI and emerging technologies presents significant challenges, these can be effectively managed through strategic planning and the adoption of innovative approaches. By addressing these challenges head-on, it is possible to create AI systems that are not only more robust and effective but also more equitable and reflective of the diverse world they are designed to serve.

Future Prospects

As the field of artificial intelligence (AI) continues to evolve, the significance of data diversity is increasingly recognized as a critical factor in the development of robust and equitable AI systems. The future of AI and emerging technologies is poised to be shaped by how effectively we can harness diverse datasets to train, validate, and test AI models. This involves not only acknowledging the importance of demographic diversity, encompassing variables such as age, gender, and ethnicity, but also understanding contextual and temporal variations that can significantly influence AI outcomes.

One of the primary challenges that lie ahead is addressing the inherent biases present in data collection processes. Historically, data collection has often underrepresented certain groups, leading to systemic biases in AI models. To mitigate these biases, future efforts must focus on inclusive data sourcing strategies that actively seek out underrepresented voices and scenarios. This can be achieved through partnerships with communities and organizations that have access to diverse data pools, thereby enriching the datasets used to train AI systems.

In addition to demographic and contextual diversity, temporal diversity plays a crucial role in ensuring that AI systems remain relevant and effective over time. As societal trends and behaviors evolve, AI models must be trained on datasets that reflect these changes to maintain accuracy and reliability. This requires ongoing data collection efforts and the establishment of frameworks for continuous learning and adaptation.

The integration of synthetic data represents another promising avenue for enhancing data diversity. By leveraging generative models, it is possible to simulate diverse scenarios and environments that may not be readily available in real-world datasets. This approach not only expands the scope of data diversity but also provides a cost-effective solution to the scarcity of high-quality, diverse datasets in specialized domains.

Looking ahead, the role of cross-domain collaboration cannot be overstated. By fostering partnerships across industries and regions, it is possible to access a wider array of datasets, each offering unique insights and perspectives. Such collaborations can drive innovation and lead to the development of AI systems that are more adaptable and resilient to edge cases. Moreover, the adoption of federated learning frameworks can enhance data diversity while maintaining privacy and security, allowing for the decentralized use of diverse data sources.

As AI systems become increasingly embedded in various aspects of daily life, ethical and governance considerations will play a pivotal role in shaping their development. Ensuring compliance with data protection regulations and fostering stakeholder engagement are essential steps in building trust and accountability. By adhering to ethical principles such as fairness, transparency, and accountability, developers can create AI systems that not only perform well across diverse scenarios but also contribute positively to society.

The future prospects of AI and emerging technologies are intrinsically linked to how well we can embrace data diversity. By addressing challenges related to bias, data availability, and ethical considerations, the field can advance towards creating AI systems that are inclusive, fair, and capable of serving the diverse needs of global populations.

This ongoing commitment to data diversity will be essential in realizing

the full potential of AI and emerging technologies in the years to come.

Chapter 13: Applications in Healthcare
Diversity in Medical Records

The integration of diversity in medical records is pivotal for the advancement of artificial intelligence (AI) and emerging technologies within the healthcare sector. Medical records hold a wealth of information that, when diverse, can significantly enhance the training and performance of AI models. Diversity in medical records encompasses a broad spectrum of variables including demographic, genetic, environmental, and socio-economic factors that reflect the complexity of human health conditions across different populations.

Incorporating diverse medical records into AI systems ensures that these technologies can cater to a wider range of healthcare needs and conditions, thereby enhancing their inclusivity and fairness. Demographic diversity, for instance, involves capturing data across various age groups, genders, ethnicities, and geographic locations. This is crucial in developing AI models that do not disproportionately favor or disadvantage any particular group, thus minimizing biases that could lead to inequitable healthcare outcomes.

Genetic diversity in medical records is equally important. With the increasing emphasis on personalized medicine, AI models require access to a variety of genetic data to predict how different individuals might respond to treatments. This genetic variability is critical for understanding the nuances of diseases and their manifestations in different genetic backgrounds, ultimately leading to more tailored and effective treatment plans.

Environmental factors also play a significant role in medical diversity. Factors such as pollution levels, climate, and urban versus rural settings can influence health outcomes. AI systems trained on medical records that include diverse environmental data are better equipped to predict and manage health issues related to these factors. This can lead to more accurate diagnostics and treatment strategies that account for environmental influences on health.

Socio-economic diversity in medical records is another crucial aspect. It involves understanding how factors such as income, education, and access to healthcare resources affect health outcomes. AI technologies that incorporate socio-economic data can help identify and address disparities in healthcare access and quality, leading to more equitable health solutions.

However, achieving diversity in medical records is not without challenges. There are significant barriers related to data collection, including privacy concerns, regulatory restrictions, and the inherent biases in existing healthcare data systems. Overcoming these challenges requires concerted efforts from policymakers, healthcare providers, and technology developers to ensure that medical records used for AI development are representative of the diverse populations they aim to serve.

The benefits of integrating diversity in medical records into AI systems are manifold. It leads to improved generalization of AI models, making them more robust and applicable to real-world healthcare scenarios. Furthermore, it enhances the resilience of these systems to rare and unexpected medical cases, thereby improving their reliability and effectiveness.

In conclusion, diversity in medical records is a cornerstone for the development of ethical, unbiased, and effective AI systems in healthcare. By focusing on this diversity, the healthcare industry can ensure that emerging technologies are well-equipped to meet the diverse needs of global populations, ultimately leading to improved health outcomes and reduced disparities in healthcare.

Improving Diagnostic Accuracy

In the realm of artificial intelligence and emerging technologies, enhancing diagnostic accuracy is a critical objective. The advent of AI has revolutionized various fields, particularly in healthcare, where diagnostic precision can significantly impact patient outcomes. The diversity of data plays a pivotal role in refining the diagnostic capabilities of AI systems, ensuring they are equipped to handle a wide range of scenarios and populations.

AI systems rely heavily on the data they are trained on. Therefore, incorporating a diverse dataset is essential to improve diagnostic accuracy. This diversity encompasses various dimensions, including demographic, contextual, temporal, and domain-specific aspects. Demographic diversity ensures that AI models are trained on data that represents different ages, genders, ethnicities, and socioeconomic statuses. This broad representation helps in creating models that do not favor any particular group, thereby minimizing biases and promoting fairness.

Contextual diversity involves training AI systems with data from various environments and cultural backgrounds, enhancing the system's adaptability to different settings. Temporal diversity, on the other hand, involves using data collected over different periods to capture trends and seasonal variations, which can be crucial in fields like epidemiology where the prevalence of diseases can change over time. Domain-specific diversity ensures that data from specialized fields, such as healthcare or manufacturing, are adequately represented, allowing AI models to perform accurately in specific contexts.

However, achieving such diversity in datasets is not without challenges. Bias in data collection, often due to systemic issues or limited access to diverse data sources, can lead to underrepresentation of certain groups. Moreover, the availability of high-quality, diverse datasets is often limited, especially in specialized domains. The cost and complexity involved in gathering and managing such datasets can also be prohibitive. Additionally, regulatory and privacy constraints pose significant challenges, particularly when dealing with sensitive data such as healthcare records.

155

Despite these challenges, the benefits of data diversity in improving diagnostic accuracy are substantial. Diverse datasets enable AI models to generalize better across different scenarios, reducing the risk of biases and ensuring fairness in decision-making. Moreover, they enhance the system's resilience to edge cases, enabling it to handle rare or unexpected inputs effectively. This capability is particularly crucial in healthcare, where diagnostic accuracy can have life-or-death implications.

To promote data diversity, several strategies can be employed. Inclusive data sourcing, which actively seeks data from underrepresented groups, is a vital approach. The use of synthetic data, generated through advanced modeling techniques, can also help simulate diverse scenarios when real-world data is scarce. Collaborations across industries and regions can facilitate access to varied datasets, while bias auditing and the use of specialized metrics can help identify and address gaps in data representation. Furthermore, federated learning offers a promising approach by leveraging decentralized data sources while maintaining privacy and security.

In conclusion, improving diagnostic accuracy through data diversity is not just a technical challenge but also an ethical imperative. By ensuring that AI systems are trained on diverse datasets, we can develop robust, fair, and effective technologies that serve the needs of a global population. This approach not only enhances the accuracy of diagnostics but also fosters innovation and trust in AI technologies.

Population Health Management

Population health management (PHM) is an approach that aims to improve the health outcomes of a group of individuals by monitoring and identifying individual patients within that group. It is an essential component of modern healthcare systems, especially as it intersects with advances in artificial intelligence (AI) and emerging technologies. By integrating data from various sources, PHM enables healthcare providers to offer more personalized and effective care, ultimately reducing costs and improving patient outcomes.

In the context of PHM, data diversity plays a crucial role. The data used in PHM must be diverse to reflect the varied demographics, lifestyles, and health conditions of the population. This diversity ensures that AI models used in PHM are inclusive and can generalize across different patient groups. The diversity of data includes demographic factors such as age, gender, ethnicity, and socioeconomic status, as well as clinical variables like medical history, genetic information, and lifestyle factors.

One of the main challenges in PHM is the integration of data from disparate sources. Healthcare data is often siloed across different institutions and formats, which can hinder comprehensive analysis. Emerging technologies, such as blockchain and cloud computing, offer solutions for secure and efficient data sharing. These technologies enable the aggregation of data from electronic health records (EHRs), wearable devices, and patient-reported outcomes, providing a holistic view of patient health.

AI and machine learning are pivotal in analyzing the vast amounts of data involved in PHM. These technologies can identify patterns and predict health outcomes, allowing for proactive interventions. For instance, AI can help in predicting hospital readmissions, identifying high-risk patients, and recommending personalized treatment plans. However, the effectiveness of these AI models is heavily dependent on the quality and diversity of the data they are trained on.

Ensuring data privacy and security is another critical aspect of PHM. With the increasing use of digital health technologies, there is a growing concern about the protection of sensitive patient information. Compliance with regulations such as the General Data Protection Regulation (GDPR) and the Health Insurance Portability and Accountability Act (HIPAA) is essential. Federated learning is one approach that addresses these concerns by enabling AI models to be trained on decentralized data, thus enhancing privacy and security.

The benefits of PHM extend beyond individual patient care. By focusing on population-level health outcomes, PHM can help identify and address public health issues, such as the management of chronic diseases and the prevention of epidemics. It also facilitates the efficient allocation of healthcare resources, ensuring that interventions are targeted where they are needed most.

In summary, population health management represents a paradigm shift in healthcare, emphasizing the integration of diverse data sources and the application of AI to improve health outcomes. As emerging technologies continue to evolve, they will play an increasingly important role in advancing PHM and achieving a more equitable and efficient healthcare system. The success of PHM relies on the continuous collaboration among healthcare providers, technology developers, and policymakers to ensure that innovations are aligned with the needs of diverse patient populations.

Case Studies

In the rapidly evolving landscape of artificial intelligence (AI) and emerging technologies, the role of data diversity has garnered significant attention. This section delves into real-world examples that illustrate the profound impact of data diversity on AI systems, highlighting both the challenges and successes encountered in various sectors.

One prominent case study involves the healthcare industry, where data diversity plays a crucial role in enhancing diagnostic accuracy. A diverse dataset encompassing various demographics, including age, gender, ethnicity, and geographic location, enables AI models to provide more accurate and inclusive diagnostic solutions. For instance, incorporating data from underrepresented populations helps in identifying and mitigating biases that could lead to misdiagnosis or inadequate treatment plans. Such efforts not only improve patient outcomes but also ensure that AI technologies adhere to ethical standards of fairness and inclusivity.

In the realm of autonomous systems, particularly self-driving cars, data diversity is indispensable for safety and adaptability. Autonomous vehicles must navigate a myriad of environments, from bustling urban centers to rural landscapes. By training AI models on diverse environmental data, developers can enhance the vehicles' ability to respond to unexpected scenarios, such as sudden weather changes or unusual traffic patterns. This diversity in training data equips autonomous systems with the resilience needed to operate safely across diverse real-world conditions.

The field of natural language processing (NLP) also benefits significantly from data diversity. Language models trained on multilingual and culturally varied datasets exhibit improved comprehension and generation capabilities. This diversity ensures that AI systems can understand and process languages with different grammatical structures, idiomatic expressions, and cultural contexts. As a result, NLP applications become more effective in delivering personalized and contextually relevant interactions for users worldwide.

In retail and marketing, data diversity empowers businesses to offer personalized experiences to a global audience. By leveraging diverse consumer data, companies can tailor their marketing strategies to resonate with different cultural preferences and purchasing behaviors.

This approach not only boosts customer engagement but also drives innovation in product development and service delivery, as businesses gain insights into the varied needs and desires of their customer base.

These case studies underscore the transformative potential of data diversity in AI and emerging technologies. However, achieving such diversity is not without its challenges. Issues related to data collection bias, availability of high-quality diverse datasets, and regulatory constraints pose significant hurdles. Addressing these challenges requires concerted efforts in inclusive data sourcing, cross-domain collaboration, and the use of synthetic data to simulate diverse scenarios. Moreover, implementing bias auditing and leveraging federated learning can further promote data diversity while ensuring privacy and security.

Ultimately, these examples highlight that data diversity is not merely a technical consideration but a foundational element in developing AI systems that are robust, ethical, and capable of serving diverse global needs effectively. By embracing data diversity, we pave the way for AI technologies that are not only innovative but also equitable and inclusive.

Future Directions

As the landscape of artificial intelligence and emerging technologies continues to evolve, the importance of data diversity becomes increasingly apparent. The future direction of this field hinges on addressing several key areas to ensure that AI systems are not only effective but also equitable and inclusive. One of the primary areas of focus is enhancing demographic diversity within datasets. This involves actively including data from a wide range of age groups, genders, ethnicities, and socioeconomic backgrounds. By doing so, AI models can be trained to better reflect and serve the diverse populations they are intended to support. Another critical aspect is ensuring contextual diversity. This means collecting and utilizing data from varied environments, whether urban or rural, and from different cultural settings. Such diversity allows AI systems to operate effectively across different scenarios and to adapt to the specific needs of various user groups. Temporal diversity is also crucial, as it involves gathering data over different time periods to capture trends and seasonal variations. This helps in building models that can predict and adapt to changes over time, which is particularly important in fields like climate science and economics. In addition to these, domain-specific diversity must be prioritized. This involves collecting data that is specific to different industries, such as healthcare, where diverse medical records can improve diagnostic accuracy and treatment outcomes. Challenges remain in achieving these diverse datasets, notably the bias in data collection, where certain groups may be underrepresented due to systemic issues or limited access to data. Overcoming these challenges requires a concerted effort to source data inclusively and ethically. The use of synthetic data is one promising approach, as it allows for the simulation of diverse scenarios in instances where real-world data may be scarce. Moreover, cross-domain collaboration is essential. By

162

partnering with organizations across various sectors and regions, there is an opportunity to access a wider range of datasets, which can enhance the robustness of AI models. Furthermore, regular bias auditing and the use of specialized metrics can help identify and address gaps in data diversity. Another innovative approach is federated learning, which leverages decentralized data sources while maintaining privacy and security. This method allows for the training of AI models on diverse datasets without the need to centralize sensitive information. In terms of applications, the future of data diversity is particularly promising in sectors such as healthcare, where diverse medical data can lead to more accurate and inclusive diagnostic tools. In the realm of autonomous systems, diverse environmental data is key to ensuring safety and adaptability. Meanwhile, in natural language processing, incorporating multilingual and culturally varied data can significantly improve the performance and inclusivity of language models. Ethical and governance considerations will also play a crucial role in guiding the future directions of data diversity. Adhering to ethical principles such as fairness, accountability, and transparency is essential. Additionally, compliance with data protection regulations, like GDPR and CCPA, is mandatory to protect individual privacy rights. Engaging stakeholders to address societal impacts and build trust is equally important. Overall, the future of data diversity in AI and emerging technologies is poised to create more robust, ethical, and impactful systems that cater to the diverse needs of global populations.

Chapter 14: Applications in Autonomous Systems
Environmental Data

In the realm of artificial intelligence and emerging technologies, the integration of environmental data plays a pivotal role in fostering innovation and enhancing the robustness of AI models. Environmental data encompasses a wide array of information gathered from various natural and human-made environments, including urban landscapes, rural settings, and extreme weather conditions. This data is crucial in training AI systems to understand and interact with the world in a manner that is both accurate and contextually relevant.

The diversity of environmental data is essential for the development of AI models that are not only effective but also equitable and inclusive. Such diversity ensures that AI systems can generalize across different settings, thereby reducing biases that might arise from a narrow focus on specific environments. For instance, training an AI model primarily on data from urban environments may lead to a system that performs suboptimally in rural or less densely populated areas. By incorporating a broad spectrum of environmental data, developers can create AI systems capable of functioning reliably across a variety of scenarios.

Moreover, the inclusion of diverse environmental data aids in the mitigation of algorithmic bias, a critical concern in the deployment of AI technologies. Bias in AI can manifest when models are trained on datasets that do not fully represent the range of conditions they will encounter in real-world applications. By ensuring that environmental data is representative of different climates, geographies, and human activities, AI systems can make fairer and more accurate predictions and decisions.

The collection and utilization of environmental data also present unique challenges. One significant challenge is the inherent variability and complexity of natural environments, which can lead to difficulties in data collection and standardization. Additionally, there are often substantial costs and logistical hurdles associated with gathering comprehensive environmental datasets, particularly in remote or underrepresented regions. These challenges necessitate innovative approaches to data collection and management, such as the use of remote sensing technologies and collaborative data-sharing frameworks.

Another important aspect of environmental data in AI is its role in enhancing the adaptability and resilience of autonomous systems. For example, self-driving cars rely heavily on environmental data to navigate safely and efficiently. By training these systems with diverse data from various driving conditions, such as different weather patterns and road types, developers can improve the vehicles' ability to handle unexpected situations and reduce the likelihood of accidents.

Furthermore, environmental data is integral to the advancement of AI applications in domains such as agriculture, where it can be used to optimize crop yields and manage natural resources more sustainably.

By analyzing patterns in environmental data, AI systems can provide farmers with actionable insights into soil health, weather forecasts, and pest control, thereby promoting more efficient and environmentally friendly agricultural practices.

In summary, environmental data serves as a cornerstone for the development of robust, fair, and innovative AI systems. Its diverse nature not only enhances the performance and generalization of AI models but also addresses critical ethical considerations by promoting inclusivity and reducing bias. As AI continues to evolve, the strategic integration of environmental data will be key to unlocking new possibilities and ensuring that AI technologies benefit society as a whole.

Safety and Adaptability

In the landscape of artificial intelligence (AI) and emerging technologies, the concepts of safety and adaptability are pivotal. These elements ensure that AI systems are not only reliable but also versatile enough to respond to the dynamic nature of real-world environments. Safety in AI refers to the system's ability to operate without causing harm to users or their surroundings. This involves rigorous testing and validation processes to identify potential risks and mitigate them before deployment.

Adaptability, on the other hand, highlights the system's ability to adjust to new and unforeseen circumstances. As AI systems are increasingly deployed in complex and unpredictable environments, their ability to learn from new data and experiences becomes crucial. This adaptability is achieved through continuous learning mechanisms, where the system refines its performance based on new inputs, thereby enhancing its functionality over time.

The integration of safety and adaptability in AI systems is especially critical in sectors such as healthcare, autonomous vehicles, and industrial automation. In healthcare, AI systems must be safe to ensure patient well-being, while also being adaptable to accommodate diverse medical conditions and patient demographics. Similarly, in autonomous vehicles, safety protocols are essential to prevent accidents, and adaptability is required to navigate varying traffic conditions and environments.

To achieve safety and adaptability, AI developers must prioritize data diversity. Diverse datasets contribute to robust AI models that can generalize well across different scenarios. This involves including data from various demographics, environments, and temporal contexts to ensure the AI system can handle a wide range of inputs and conditions. Moreover, incorporating feedback loops where AI systems learn from user interactions and real-world experiences can further enhance their adaptability.

Ethical considerations also play a significant role in the development of safe and adaptable AI systems. Ensuring compliance with ethical standards and legal regulations, such as data protection laws, is essential to maintain public trust and prevent misuse. Additionally, transparency in AI decision-making processes can help users understand how systems adapt and operate, fostering a sense of security and reliability.

The balance between safety and adaptability also involves trade-offs. Systems that are overly focused on safety may become rigid and unable to adapt to new situations, while those that prioritize adaptability may introduce risks if changes are not carefully managed. Therefore, achieving an optimal balance requires a nuanced approach that considers the specific needs and contexts of the application.

In conclusion, safety and adaptability are integral to the successful deployment of AI systems in emerging technologies. By leveraging data diversity, ethical practices, and continuous learning, developers can create AI solutions that are both secure and flexible, capable of meeting the challenges of today's dynamic world.

Real-World Challenges

In the realm of artificial intelligence and emerging technologies, the pursuit of data diversity presents a multitude of real-world challenges that must be navigated to create inclusive and effective AI systems. One of the primary challenges is the inherent bias in data collection processes. Often, data is collected from sources that do not adequately represent the full spectrum of societal demographics, leading to underrepresentation of certain groups or scenarios. This bias can stem from systemic issues or simply from limited access to diverse data sources. As a result, AI models trained on such data may fail to perform equitably across different populations.

Data availability further complicates the quest for diversity, especially in specialized domains where high-quality, diverse datasets are scarce. This scarcity is often due to the sensitive nature of the data or the logistical challenges involved in collecting it. The cost and complexity of gathering and managing diverse datasets also pose significant hurdles. Organizations must invest substantial resources into sourcing, storing, and processing these datasets, which can be a deterrent, especially for smaller entities or those operating in resource-constrained environments.

Moreover, regulatory and privacy constraints present additional barriers. Legal frameworks such as the General Data Protection Regulation (GDPR) and the California Consumer Privacy Act (CCPA) impose strict guidelines on data usage, particularly when it involves sensitive or protected information. These regulations, while essential for protecting individual privacy, can limit the accessibility of diverse datasets necessary for training robust AI systems.

Despite these challenges, the benefits of achieving data diversity are manifold. Diverse datasets enhance the generalization capabilities of AI models, enabling them to perform more effectively across a wide array of real-world scenarios. This reduction in algorithmic bias not only ensures fairness in decision-making but also fosters innovation by inspiring novel applications and insights. Furthermore, systems trained on diverse data are more resilient to edge cases, equipping them to handle rare or unexpected inputs with greater efficacy.

To overcome these challenges, several strategies can be employed. Inclusive data sourcing is crucial, necessitating active efforts to gather data from underrepresented groups and contexts. When real-world data is limited, synthetic data generation can simulate diverse scenarios, providing an alternative pathway to achieving data diversity. Cross-domain collaboration also plays a vital role, as partnerships with organizations across different industries and regions can facilitate access to varied datasets.

Bias auditing and the use of specialized metrics are essential for regularly evaluating datasets for gaps and biases. These tools help ensure that datasets remain representative and equitable. Federated learning presents another solution, allowing organizations to leverage decentralized data sources while maintaining privacy and security. By addressing these real-world challenges, the field of AI and emerging technologies can move towards creating systems that are not only technically advanced but also socially responsible and ethically sound.

Enhancements through Diversity

In the rapidly evolving realm of artificial intelligence and emerging technologies, diversity in data is a cornerstone for progress and innovation. By incorporating a wide array of data sources, AI systems can be designed to be more inclusive, fair, and effective across different populations and scenarios. This diversity encompasses several dimensions, including demographics, contexts, time periods, and domain-specific variations, each contributing to the robustness and adaptability of AI models.

Demographic diversity is crucial as it includes variables such as age, gender, ethnicity, socioeconomic status, and geographic location. By ensuring that datasets reflect these diverse attributes, AI models can better generalize across different groups, reducing bias and enhancing the fairness of decision-making processes. Contextual diversity, on the other hand, involves capturing variations in environments and use cases, such as urban versus rural settings or cultural differences, which are vital for creating AI systems that are adaptable to various real-world situations.

Temporal diversity is another important aspect, as it involves collecting data over different time periods to capture trends and seasonal variations. This is particularly important in applications that require an understanding of temporal dynamics, such as financial forecasting or climate modeling. Domain-specific diversity refers to the inclusion of varied industry-specific data, which is essential for tailoring AI solutions to specific sectors like healthcare, manufacturing, or education.

However, achieving data diversity is not without challenges. There are inherent biases in data collection processes, often resulting from systemic issues or limited access to diverse data sources. Additionally, the scarcity of high-quality, diverse datasets in specialized domains poses a significant barrier. The cost and complexity associated with gathering and managing such datasets can also be prohibitive, not to mention the regulatory and privacy constraints that must be navigated to ensure ethical data use.

Despite these challenges, the benefits of data diversity are manifold. Diverse datasets improve the generalization of AI models, enabling them to perform better across a range of real-world scenarios. They also play a crucial role in bias mitigation, ensuring that AI systems are more equitable and just in their operations. Furthermore, access to broad datasets can inspire innovative applications and insights, driving the development of novel technologies and solutions.

To promote data diversity, several strategies can be employed. Actively sourcing data from underrepresented groups and contexts is one approach, while synthetic data generation can be utilized to simulate diverse scenarios when real-world data is insufficient. Cross-domain collaboration can also provide access to varied datasets, enhancing the diversity of data inputs. Regular auditing for biases and gaps, using specialized tools and frameworks, is essential to maintain the integrity and fairness of datasets. Federated learning offers a decentralized approach to leveraging diverse data sources while ensuring privacy and security.

Incorporating data diversity into AI systems is not just a technical necessity but an ethical imperative. By adhering to ethical principles such as fairness, accountability, and transparency, and ensuring compliance with data protection regulations, stakeholders can foster trust and engagement with these technologies. Ultimately, data diversity is foundational for creating robust, ethical, and impactful AI systems that effectively serve diverse global needs.

Future Prospects

The landscape of data diversity in AI and emerging technologies holds significant potential for future developments. As the world becomes increasingly interconnected, the demand for AI systems that can operate seamlessly across diverse environments intensifies. This necessitates an expansion in the scope and application of data diversity, pushing boundaries in AI research and development.

One of the foremost prospects is the enhancement of AI model robustness through enriched data diversity. By incorporating a wider array of datasets that reflect various demographic characteristics, environmental conditions, and temporal changes, AI systems can achieve improved generalization. This means that these systems will be better equipped to perform accurately in a multitude of real-world scenarios, reducing the prevalence of bias and enhancing fairness in automated decision-making processes.

Moreover, the future of data diversity in AI is closely tied to advancements in synthetic data generation. As real-world data collection continues to face challenges such as privacy concerns and logistical constraints, synthetic data offers a viable alternative. Techniques such as generative adversarial networks (GANs) can create realistic and varied data sets that mimic real-world diversity without the associated risks of data breaches or ethical violations. This advancement not only mitigates data scarcity issues but also provides a controlled environment for testing AI models under diverse conditions.

Cross-domain collaborations will likely play a pivotal role in the future landscape of data diversity. By forming partnerships across different industries and geographic regions, organizations can gain access to a broader spectrum of data. Such collaborations can foster innovation and lead to the development of more comprehensive AI solutions that address global challenges. For instance, in the healthcare sector, sharing diverse medical data across borders can enhance the accuracy of predictive models, ultimately improving patient outcomes worldwide.

Furthermore, the integration of federated learning frameworks presents a promising avenue for the future. Federated learning allows AI models to be trained on decentralized data sources, maintaining data privacy while still benefiting from diverse datasets. This approach can significantly enhance the ability of AI systems to learn from a wide range of data inputs, thereby improving their adaptability and performance across different contexts.

As data diversity continues to evolve, ethical and governance considerations will remain at the forefront. Ensuring that AI systems adhere to principles of fairness, accountability, and transparency is crucial in building public trust and acceptance. This involves not only compliance with existing data protection regulations but also proactive engagement with stakeholders to address societal impacts and ethical dilemmas associated with AI deployment.

In summary, the future prospects of data diversity in AI and emerging technologies are vast and multifaceted. By embracing innovations in synthetic data, cross-domain collaborations, and federated learning, the AI community can develop more inclusive and effective systems. As these technologies advance, they hold the promise of transforming industries and improving lives globally, provided that ethical considerations are diligently addressed.

Chapter 15: Future of Data Diversity in AI
Evolving Technologies

The rapid advancement of technology is reshaping the landscape of artificial intelligence (AI) and emerging technologies. This evolution is fueled by the increasing availability of diverse data and the sophisticated algorithms that process it. As technology progresses, it integrates more deeply into various aspects of human life, creating systems that are more capable, adaptable, and intelligent.

At the core of these advancements is the concept of data diversity, which refers to the variety in data used to train, validate, and test AI models. This diversity encompasses demographic factors such as age, gender, and ethnicity, as well as contextual elements like environment and culture. By incorporating a wide range of data, AI systems can achieve improved generalization, making them more effective across different real-world scenarios.

One of the primary challenges in evolving technologies is ensuring that AI systems are inclusive and fair. Bias in data collection often leads to the underrepresentation of certain groups, which can result in biased algorithms. This issue is compounded by the scarcity of diverse, high-quality datasets in specialized domains. Addressing these challenges requires concerted efforts in inclusive data sourcing and the use of synthetic data to simulate diverse scenarios when real-world data is limited.

The benefits of embracing data diversity are manifold. It leads to better generalization of AI models, reduces algorithmic bias, and fosters innovation by inspiring novel applications and insights. Furthermore, systems become more resilient to edge cases, handling rare or unexpected inputs with greater efficiency. Techniques such as federated learning allow for leveraging decentralized data sources while maintaining privacy and security, thus enhancing data diversity without compromising ethical standards.

In the realm of emerging technologies, data diversity plays a crucial role in various applications. In healthcare, diverse medical records improve diagnostic accuracy across different populations, ensuring that healthcare solutions are equitable and effective. Autonomous systems, such as self-driving cars, benefit from diverse environmental data, which enhances their safety and adaptability in various conditions. Similarly, natural language processing (NLP) systems improve when exposed to multilingual and culturally varied data, making them more robust in understanding and generating human language.

The integration of diverse data into emerging technologies also extends to retail and marketing, where it enables personalized experiences for global audiences. By understanding the preferences and behaviors of diverse consumer groups, businesses can tailor their offerings to meet the specific needs of individuals across different regions.

It is imperative to adhere to ethical principles such as fairness, accountability, and transparency in the deployment of AI and emerging technologies. Compliance with data protection regulations, such as GDPR and CCPA, is essential to protect individual privacy and build trust with stakeholders. Engaging with these stakeholders helps address societal impacts and fosters the responsible development of technology.

Overall, the evolution of technology in AI and related fields underscores the importance of data diversity. By harnessing this diversity, we can create AI systems that are robust, ethical, and impactful, effectively serving the diverse needs of global populations.

Integration with AI

The integration of artificial intelligence (AI) into diverse technological domains has become a pivotal aspect of modern innovation. This integration is not merely about embedding AI capabilities into existing systems but involves a comprehensive approach to enhancing functionalities and creating synergies between AI and other technologies. The multifaceted nature of AI integration encompasses several key dimensions, each contributing to the overall effectiveness and efficiency of technological solutions.

One of the primary dimensions of AI integration is the enhancement of decision-making processes. AI systems, with their advanced data processing and analytical capabilities, provide unparalleled insights that drive informed decision-making across various sectors. For instance, in healthcare, AI-powered analytics can process vast amounts of medical data to support diagnostic and treatment decisions, thereby improving patient outcomes and reducing human error.

Furthermore, AI integration facilitates automation, which is transforming industries by streamlining operations and increasing productivity. Automation, powered by AI, extends beyond routine tasks and includes complex processes that were traditionally dependent on human intervention. In manufacturing, for example, AI-driven automation can optimize supply chain management, predict maintenance needs, and enhance quality control, leading to more efficient production cycles and reduced operational costs.

Another critical aspect of AI integration is the personalization of user experiences. AI technologies enable systems to learn from user interactions and preferences, tailoring services and products to meet individual needs. This personalization is evident in e-commerce, where AI algorithms analyze customer behavior to recommend products, thus enhancing customer satisfaction and increasing sales.

AI integration also plays a significant role in enhancing cybersecurity measures. As cyber threats become more sophisticated, AI systems are deployed to detect and respond to potential threats in real-time. These systems can analyze patterns and anomalies in network traffic, providing robust defense mechanisms against cyberattacks. This proactive approach to cybersecurity ensures the protection of sensitive data and critical infrastructure.

Moreover, the integration of AI into emerging technologies fosters innovation and the development of new applications. AI's ability to process and analyze large datasets opens up possibilities for advancements in fields such as natural language processing, image recognition, and autonomous systems. In autonomous vehicles, AI integration enables real-time decision-making and navigation, enhancing safety and efficiency on the roads.

The integration process, however, is not without its challenges. Ensuring data diversity is crucial to the development of AI systems that are fair and unbiased. Diverse datasets are necessary to train AI models that are representative of various demographic and contextual scenarios, thus minimizing bias and improving the robustness of AI applications.

Additionally, ethical considerations must be addressed in AI integration. Adhering to principles of fairness, accountability, and transparency is essential to building trust and acceptance among stakeholders. Compliance with data protection regulations, such as GDPR and CCPA, is also vital to safeguard user privacy and maintain ethical standards in AI deployment.

In summary, the integration of AI into diverse technological domains is a complex yet rewarding endeavor that enhances capabilities, drives innovation, and addresses contemporary challenges. By focusing on data diversity, ethical considerations, and the synergies between AI and other technologies, we can harness the full potential of AI to create solutions that are both effective and inclusive.

Global Impact

The transformative power of data diversity is reshaping how artificial intelligence (AI) and emerging technologies operate on a global scale. As AI systems are increasingly embedded in various societal facets, the call for diverse datasets becomes imperative to ensure these systems are inclusive, fair, and effective across a wide range of populations. This requires embracing the complexities of demographic, contextual, temporal, and domain-specific diversity in data.

Demographic diversity encompasses variations in age, gender, ethnicity, socioeconomic status, and geographic location. These aspects ensure that AI models are trained on data that represents the full spectrum of human experiences, minimizing biases that could lead to unfair treatment or misrepresentation. Similarly, contextual diversity considers variations in environments, cultures, and use cases, enabling AI systems to adapt and function efficiently in both urban and rural settings, across different cultural contexts, and in varied scenarios.

Temporal diversity is crucial for capturing trends and seasonality, ensuring that AI models remain relevant and accurate over time. This type of diversity involves collecting data across different periods, which helps in understanding and predicting changes in patterns and behaviors. Domain-specific diversity, on the other hand, refers to the inclusion of data from specific industries like healthcare, manufacturing, or education, each with its unique requirements and challenges. This diversity ensures that AI applications are tailored to meet industry-specific needs efficiently.

The global impact of data diversity is profound, influencing not just the technical performance of AI systems but also their societal acceptance and ethical implications. By integrating diverse datasets, AI systems can improve their generalization capabilities, making them more resilient to edge cases and better equipped to handle rare or unexpected inputs. This leads to enhanced innovation, as a broader range of data inspires new applications and insights, driving technological advancement across sectors.

Moreover, data diversity plays a pivotal role in bias mitigation. By reducing algorithmic bias, AI systems can ensure fairness in decision-making processes, which is crucial in applications like recruitment, lending, or law enforcement, where biased outcomes can have significant societal repercussions. This aspect of fairness is not just a technical challenge but an ethical mandate, requiring adherence to principles of accountability and transparency.

Promoting data diversity involves strategic approaches such as inclusive data sourcing, which actively seeks data from underrepresented groups and contexts. The use of synthetic data is another strategy, where generative models simulate diverse scenarios when real-world data is scarce. Cross-domain collaboration is also vital, as partnerships with organizations across different industries and regions can provide access to varied datasets, enriching the AI training process.

Federated learning emerges as a promising approach to leverage decentralized data sources while maintaining privacy and security, a critical consideration in today's data-driven world. This method allows for the aggregation of insights without the direct exchange of data, preserving individual privacy while still benefiting from the diversity of decentralized data.

In conclusion, the integration of data diversity within AI and emerging technologies is not merely a technical requirement but a foundational element for creating robust, ethical, and impactful systems. These systems are poised to serve diverse global needs effectively, fostering trust and acceptance in the communities they aim to benefit.

Challenges Ahead

As the field of artificial intelligence (AI) and emerging technologies continues to evolve, addressing the challenges of data diversity is becoming increasingly critical. Data diversity encompasses a wide range of elements, including demographic, contextual, temporal, and domain-specific diversity. Each of these elements contributes to the robustness and inclusivity of AI systems, which in turn impact their effectiveness across various applications.

One of the primary challenges in achieving data diversity is the inherent bias present in data collection processes. Often, certain groups or scenarios are underrepresented due to systemic issues or limited access to diverse data sources. This underrepresentation can lead to biased AI models, which may not perform well across all populations or scenarios. To mitigate this, it is essential to actively seek data from underrepresented groups and contexts, ensuring that the data used to train AI models is as inclusive as possible.

Another significant challenge is the availability of diverse, high-quality datasets, particularly in specialized domains. In many cases, there is a scarcity of such datasets, which can hinder the development of AI models that are capable of generalizing across a wide range of scenarios. To address this, the use of synthetic data, generated through advanced generative models, can be a valuable strategy. This approach allows for the simulation of diverse scenarios, providing a broader dataset for training AI systems when real-world data is limited.

The cost and complexity associated with gathering and managing diverse datasets also present substantial challenges. Collecting data from a wide variety of sources can be resource-intensive, requiring significant investments in both time and money. This complexity is further compounded by regulatory and privacy constraints, which impose legal and ethical considerations on the access and use of sensitive or protected data. Navigating these constraints requires a careful balance between innovation and compliance, ensuring that data diversity efforts adhere to relevant regulations while still fostering the development of robust AI systems.

Despite these challenges, the benefits of data diversity are profound. Diverse datasets lead to improved generalization of AI models, enabling them to perform effectively across a range of real-world scenarios. This not only reduces algorithmic bias but also ensures fairness in decision-making processes. Additionally, access to a wider variety of data can enhance innovation, inspiring novel applications and insights that may not have been possible with more homogeneous datasets.

Furthermore, data diversity contributes to the resilience of AI systems, equipping them to handle rare or unexpected inputs more effectively. This resilience is particularly important in applications such as healthcare and autonomous systems, where the ability to adapt to diverse environments and populations is crucial for safety and efficacy.

In conclusion, while there are significant challenges associated with achieving data diversity in AI and emerging technologies, the potential benefits make these efforts worthwhile. By prioritizing inclusive data sourcing, leveraging synthetic data, and fostering cross-domain collaboration, the field can move towards more equitable and effective AI systems that serve the diverse needs of a global population.

Vision for the Future

The future landscape of data diversity in artificial intelligence and emerging technologies holds significant promise for advancing inclusivity and fairness in AI systems. As technology continues to evolve, the need for diverse data sets becomes increasingly critical to ensure that AI models can effectively serve a global audience. The vision for the future in this context revolves around addressing current challenges while leveraging new opportunities to enhance data diversity.

One of the primary challenges today is the inherent bias present in many data collection processes. This bias often stems from systemic issues that result in the underrepresentation of certain groups or scenarios. Moving forward, it is crucial to develop methodologies that actively mitigate these biases. This will involve creating frameworks for inclusive data sourcing that prioritize the representation of diverse demographics, languages, and cultural contexts. By doing so, AI systems can be trained to be more equitable and effective across different populations.

Another aspect of the future vision involves overcoming the scarcity of diverse, high-quality datasets. This can be achieved by fostering cross-domain collaborations and partnerships with organizations across various industries and regions. Such collaborations can facilitate access to a broader range of data sources, enabling the development of AI models that are more robust and resilient to edge cases.

Additionally, the use of synthetic data generated through advanced generative models can simulate diverse scenarios, providing a viable alternative when real-world data is limited.

The future also envisions the integration of federated learning approaches, which allow for decentralized data processing. This method not only enhances data diversity but also addresses privacy and security concerns by keeping data localized while still contributing to the training of global AI models. Federated learning can thus play a pivotal role in advancing data diversity without compromising user privacy.

In the realm of emerging technologies, data diversity will be instrumental in driving innovation and improving the functionality of AI applications. For instance, in healthcare, diverse datasets can lead to more accurate diagnostics and treatments tailored to varied populations. In autonomous systems, diverse environmental data can enhance the adaptability and safety of vehicles operating in different geographic locations. Similarly, in natural language processing, incorporating multilingual and culturally varied data can significantly improve the performance of language models, making them more accessible and useful worldwide.

Ethical and governance considerations will remain at the forefront of advancing data diversity. Ensuring compliance with data protection regulations, such as GDPR and CCPA, will be essential to maintaining public trust and accountability. Engaging stakeholders in the development and deployment of AI systems will also help address societal impacts and foster a more inclusive technological ecosystem.

The vision for the future of data diversity in AI and emerging technologies is one of continuous improvement and adaptation. By addressing current challenges and embracing innovative strategies, the potential for AI systems to become more inclusive, fair, and effective is vast. This future-focused approach will not only enhance the capabilities of AI but also ensure that these technologies serve the diverse needs of a global society.

EPILOGUE

As we reflect on the insights presented in this book, it is clear that the path forward in AI and emerging technologies is intricately tied to embracing data diversity. By acknowledging the multifaceted nature of data, we can build systems that are not only technically advanced but also ethically sound and socially responsible. The importance of demographic, contextual, temporal, and domain-specific diversity cannot be overstated, as these elements collectively ensure that AI systems are fair, inclusive, and truly representative of the global population.

The challenges in achieving data diversity, such as bias in data collection and scarcity of diverse datasets, highlight the need for innovative solutions and collaborative efforts across industries. Strategies like inclusive data sourcing, synthetic data generation, and federated learning are vital in overcoming these obstacles and paving the way for more equitable AI systems.

Moreover, the benefits of data diversity extend beyond just technical performance. They encompass improved generalization, bias mitigation, enhanced innovation, and resilience to edge cases, which are crucial for the sustainable development of AI technologies. These benefits underscore the need for a concerted effort to incorporate diverse data in AI development processes.

As we move forward, it is essential to adhere to ethical principles and governance frameworks that prioritize fairness, accountability, and transparency. By doing so, we can build AI systems that not only meet the technical demands of the future but also align with the societal values of equity and justice. This book serves as a call to action for all stakeholders in the AI ecosystem to prioritize data diversity and work towards creating a future where AI systems serve diverse global needs effectively.

ABOUT THE AUTHOR

Dr. Ivan Del Valle is an International Business Transformation Executive with extensive senior leadership experience in strategy and management consulting at top firms like Accenture and Capgemini. He led the data integration for one of the largest touchless planning and fulfillment implementations in the world for a $346 billion healthcare company. Born and raised on the picturesque Caribbean island of Puerto Rico, he currently resides with his beloved wife and Cavalier King Charles Spaniels in the historic district of Charleston, South Carolina, in the United States.

He earned a Ph.D. in Law from Apsley Business School in London, UK, focusing his research on the laws and regulations pertaining to the legal aspects of blockchain-driven international trade traceability in sustainable food chains. On his current role as a Global Enterprise Data & Analytics Executive at Boston Scientific, he spearheads a broad range of initiatives across Data Engineering and Machine Learning/AI. His proficiency pioneering the development of Generative AI use cases within the Medical Devices sector as an integral part of the Life Sciences industry is internationally recognized. His leadership in these innovative areas underscores a commitment to advancing data analytics and AI applications in healthcare technology.

In addition to his hands-on, value driven credentials, Dr. Del Valle holds an MBA from the University of The People in Pasadena,

California, a Master's in Data Science & Analytics from the prestigious Nebrija University in Madrid, Spain, and a Master's degree in Consumer Neuroscience (Neuromarketing) from UNIR Mexico. He lectures at Apsley Business School London, covering Applied AI Advanced topics, International & Comparative Law, Strategic Management and Organizational Theory, and is a regular panel participant in leading-edge, international, multi-industry conferences.

Dr. Del Valle can be reached via LinkedIn at
https://www.linkedin.com/in/enterprise-solutions

www.ingramcontent.com/pod-product-compliance
Lightning Source LLC
LaVergne TN
LVHW041210050326
832903LV00021B/564